SHADES OF THE SOUL

A Devotional Journey Through
Strength
Hope
and
Transformation

Neisha Vincent

Disclaimer:

This devotional is intended for personal growth and spiritual reflection and is not a substitute for professional advice, counseling, or therapy. The reflections and insights shared are the author's interpretations and may not represent official teachings of any religious organization.

Scripture quotations marked NIV are taken from the Holy Bible, New International Version®, NIV®. Copyright © 1973, 1978, 1984, 2011 by Biblica, Inc.® Used by permission. All rights reserved worldwide.

While every effort has been made to ensure accuracy, please refer to the Bible directly for any in-depth study.

Step into the beauty of a life transformed by Christ, where every step you take is guided by His love, every burden lightened by His grace. Imagine a journey where peace replaces worry, where kindness flows like a river, and where your spirit awakens to a purpose far greater than yourself. In Christ, we find a love that heals the broken places within us, a joy that lifts us beyond our struggles, and a hope that speaks to the deepest parts of who we are.

Walking with Christ is not just a path; it is a dance of faith and freedom, where every trial becomes a lesson, every moment a chance to love more deeply, more fully. His love calls us not to merely exist, but to live abundantly, to walk in the light and share that light with all who cross our path. Come, draw closer, and experience the goodness of a life lived in step with the One who calls you beloved. Let your heart be transformed and your spirit renewed, for in His love, you will find the strength to walk boldly, to love freely, and to live fully.

God's love for us is beyond measure—immeasurable, unstoppable, unconditional. He doesn't just see us as we are. He loves us as we are, imperfections and all. "While we were still sinners, Christ died for us" (Romans 5:8). You don't need to be perfect for His love, and He calls you to live your best life, guided by that love.

Just as He loves us, we're called to love one another. "As I have loved you, so you must love one another" (John 13:34). This isn't just a suggestion; it's a calling, a way of living. Even when others fall short, even when people don't treat you right, you have the power to rise above. Love anyway. Because the love you give has the power to change hearts, just as God's love has transformed yours. That's how we reflect God's heart and live a life that truly matters. Step into that love today.

Hearing the Voice of God

"My sheep listen to my voice; I know them, and they follow me."
— John 10:27 (NIV)

This is so powerful and so essential for your life—hearing the voice of God. You are His sheep. You are His beloved, and He is speaking to you every day, guiding you, leading you, and calling you into the life He's designed for you.

God's voice is always calling. But in the race of life, we let the world's noise—distractions, worries, even our own doubts—drown it out. Yet, here's the truth: Jesus says His sheep know His voice. You don't have to wonder if God's talking to you—He is! Right now. He knows you. He knows your heart. And He's leading you, pushing you forward, driving you toward the purpose He's created just for you. It's time to tune out the noise, lock in, and follow the voice that's been calling your name since day one. This is your moment. Let nothing hold you back!

Take Moses, for example. When God first called Moses from the burning bush, Moses was uncertain, hesitant, and full of doubt. He felt unworthy, unqualified, and overwhelmed. God didn't choose Moses because he was perfect—He chose Moses because he was willing to listen. Moses could have walked away from that burning bush; he could have ignored the voice of God. But instead, he leaned in and heard what God was calling him to do. And because Moses listened, he led an entire nation out of captivity.

What is God calling you to do today? Maybe you're standing at the edge of your own burning bush moment, unsure if you're ready, questioning whether you have what it takes. Let me tell you—God doesn't make mistakes! If He's calling you, it's because He's already equipped you with everything you need. You don't need to have it all figured out. Just listen to His voice and trust Him. When you follow His lead, He'll unlock doors that no one can shut, carve a path where there seems to be none, and stay by your side every step of the journey. This is your moment. Step into it!

Father, thank You for speaking my name and calling me to greatness. Help me to hear Your voice in every moment and trust that You're leading me. I choose to follow with boldness, knowing Your plan is unstoppable and perfect for my life. In Jesus' name, amen.

Encouragement

Be encouraged that God knows you, He sees you, and He is speaking to you. As you tune your heart to His voice, He will guide you in every decision and every step you take. You are not alone—your Good Shepherd is with you, leading you to green pastures and still waters. Listen for His voice, follow His lead, and watch how He transforms your life into something beautiful beyond your imagination!

Called to stand out

"But you are a chosen people, a royal priesthood, a holy nation, God's special possession, that you may declare the praises of him who called you out of darkness into his wonderful light."
1 Peter 2:9 (NIV)

Have you ever felt like you just don't fit in? That's because God didn't call you to blend in—He called you to stand out! Look at Daniel, taken captive in a foreign land, surrounded by a culture trying to shape him. He could've gone along with the crowd, but Daniel stood firm in his faith. He refused to compromise, because he knew who he was—a child of the Most High God. And what happened? God honored him, gave him favor, and made him a light in the darkness. Even in the lion's den, Daniel stood strong, and God delivered him. You're not meant to fit in—you're meant to shine. Stand out, because that's what you were made for! You are a flame in a world of shadows, meant to burn brightly with a purpose only you can fulfill.

The power of favor sets you apart in ways that human effort alone never could. It's the undeniable hand of God, opening doors that seemed locked and making ways where there were none. Your faithfulness aligns you with God's purpose and positions you to impact others in powerful ways. Favor doesn't mean life will be easy, but it means that God's strength will carry you through challenges and lift you above limitations. When God's favor is on your life, even the impossible becomes possible. You weren't created to blend in; you were made to be remarkable—go out and embrace it.

Ask yourself : Am I living to fit in, or am I living to stand out for Christ? Don't be afraid to be different.

Claim your identity in Christ, shatter the mold, and let your radiant spirit light up the world—because when you know who you are, there's no stopping you. Embrace the beauty of being set apart, knowing that your uniqueness is part of His perfect design. Every moment you choose to stand out for Christ, you're shining a light that reaches beyond yourself. Discover the confidence of living in purpose—radiant, authentic, and truly you.

Father, thank You for calling me to stand out in this world. Help me to embrace my identity as part of Your royal priesthood and to live in a way that reflects Your light and love. Give me the courage to stand firm in my faith, even when it feels uncomfortable or lonely. I trust that You have chosen me for a purpose and that my life can bring glory to Your name. In Jesus' name, Amen.

Encouragement

Remember, you're not like everyone else—and that's your greatest strength. Just like Daniel, you've been called to be different, to be a reflection of greatness. Don't settle for fitting in when you were born to shine. Stand tall in your purpose, live boldly with conviction, and let your life tell the story of unstoppable determination. You were made to stand out, so own it and show the world what you're made of!

Jesus, The Way, The Truth, and The Life

"Jesus answered, 'I am the way and the truth and the life. No one comes to the Father except through me.'"
— John 14:6 (NIV)

Jesus makes one of the most profound declarations in all of Scripture. He isn't just pointing us in the right direction—He "is" the way. He doesn't just teach us the truth—He "is" the truth. And He doesn't just offer us life—He "is" the life. Everything you need for peace, purpose, and salvation is found in Him. In His embrace, all paths converge, all questions dissolve, and in His light, the soul finds its eternal home. To walk with Him is to journey beyond fear, stepping into a love that holds the universe together.

Think about Thomas, the disciple who was struggling to understand what Jesus meant about going to the Father. He asked Jesus, "How can we know the way?" (John 14:5). Maybe you've felt like Thomas, wondering which path to take, or confused about what the future holds. But here's the beauty of it—Jesus didn't just leave Thomas in confusion. He responded with assurance: "I am the way." Jesus was telling Thomas, "You don't need to figure out all the steps. Just follow Me, and I will lead you."

Look at Paul—he thought he had it all figured out, convinced he knew the way. But on the road to Damascus, everything changed. When he met Jesus, he found the real Way, the Truth, and the Life. Paul didn't just adjust his plans—he transformed his life, going from persecutor to preacher, leading countless people to Christ. That's the power of John 14:6. When you follow Jesus, everything changes. Step into it!

Jesus never promised an easy road, but He promised to be *the* way through every battle. When you follow Him, you're not lost—you're driven by purpose. His truth anchors you, keeping you steady against the world's lies. And when you embrace the life He gives, you're not just surviving—you're thriving, filled with hope, joy, and the power to conquer anything that stands in your way.

Father, thank You for sending Jesus as the Way, the Truth, and the Life. Help me to trust Him completely, knowing that when I follow Him, I'm stepping into Your perfect plan. Light my path, reveal Your truth in every moment, and ignite my life with Your purpose. In Jesus' name, amen.

Encouragement

If you're feeling lost or unsure, remember this: Jesus *is* the way. You don't need to figure it all out—just trust Him, step by step. In a world full of confusion, He *is* the truth, and He won't let you down. Looking for purpose? Jesus *is* the life. Everything you need is in Him. You're not alone on this journey. Just like Paul's life was transformed, so will yours. Keep your eyes on Jesus, walk in His truth, live His life, and step into victory. Trust Him—your future is filled with His promises!

A New Creation in Christ

Life has a way of making us feel stuck sometimes, doesn't it? Whether it's the mistakes we've made, the baggage we carry, or just the daily grind, we all have moments when we feel like we're dragging our old selves around. But here's the good news: the Bible tells us in 2 Corinthians 5:17 that when you are in Christ, you are a new creation. That's not just a fresh coat of paint—it's a complete renovation! The old is gone, and the new has come.

Zacchaeus was a tax collector, a man often disliked by his community because of his role in collecting taxes—often unfairly—from his fellow citizens. Despite his wealth, he was spiritually empty and desperate for change. When Jesus passed through Jericho, Zacchaeus, being short in stature, climbed a tree to catch a glimpse of Him. To everyone's surprise, Jesus called Zacchaeus by name and invited Himself to his home. This encounter changed Zacchaeus completely. He repented and committed to giving half of his wealth to the poor, as well as paying back anyone he had wronged. His story perfectly relates to 2 Corinthians 5:17 because it demonstrates how an encounter with Jesus makes us a new creation—Zacchaeus was transformed from a sinner to someone living out a new, redeemed identity. The old Zacchaeus was gone, and the new had come!

You are not your past. In Christ, you are a new creation. Zacchaeus climbed that tree as a broken man, but when Jesus called him down, everything changed. Just like that, your mistakes, your failures—they don't define you anymore. Jesus transforms you from the inside out.

The old is gone, the new is here! Step into that newness with confidence. You're not just patched up; you're completely new.

Today is your moment. So, how do we live this out? Stop dragging around the past. Walk in the identity Christ gave you, and leave your past behind. If God has declared you new, believe it. Let go of the guilt, the shame, and the failures of yesterday, and step into the new identity Christ has given you. Remind yourself that you are not who you used to be. You are a new creation, and God's power is at work in you. Stand firm in your new identity. Like Zacchaeus, you are no longer defined by what you've done but by who Jesus says you are.

Father, thank You for making me a new creation in Christ. Help me to let go of my past and embrace the future You have for me. I trust that Your transformation is real, and I choose to live in the freedom and identity You've given me. Thank You for the grace that makes all things new. In Jesus' name, Amen.

Encouragement

You are brand new! Not repaired, not patched up—you are a completely transformed creation in Christ. Your past? It has no power over you anymore. Just like Zacchaeus, your story has been rewritten, and now you're stepping into a future filled with purpose and potential. It's time to own that truth, move with confidence, and embrace the life God has prepared for you. The old is behind you—the new is here! Walk in it with boldness and victory! This is your season to shine, unburdened and unstoppable. Embrace the transformation, live fully, and let the world see the new creation you were always meant to be.

Strength in the Lord

*Finally, be strong in the Lord
and in his mighty power."
~Ephesians 6:10 (NIV)*

This isn't just a call to rely on our own strength; it's an invitation to tap into God's boundless power. Paul knew the weight of this command—he was writing to believers who faced intense persecution, reminding them that God's power was their greatest weapon. When the world feels overwhelming, and our strength falls short, this verse reminds us that we don't have to face life's battles alone. True strength isn't about what we can do by ourselves; it's about leaning into the limitless might of the Lord.

Think about a soldier gearing up for battle. They don't just walk onto the battlefield in ordinary clothes; they put on armor, knowing it will shield them and give them confidence to face what's ahead. Our spiritual journey is much like this. When we're up against challenges—whether it's a demanding job, financial struggles, or conflict in relationships—we often try to push through on our own, only to feel drained and defeated. But God tells us to "be strong in the Lord," to put on His strength as our armor. This is the strength that doesn't waver when circumstances are rough, a power that carries us when we feel weak. Just like a soldier's armor protects from external threats, God's strength shields us from the doubts and fears that try to penetrate our hearts. When we wear His strength, we're not just defending ourselves; we're empowered to advance, to overcome, and to thrive even in the toughest battles. His strength is a steady foundation, a force that lifts us beyond our own limits and enables us to face each day with courage. God's power isn't just support; it's transformation, turning moments of weakness into victories.

With His strength as your armor, step forward—unstoppable, unbreakable, and ready for anything. Today, start by acknowledging your need for God's strength. Let go of the pressure to handle everything yourself and invite God into the challenges you face. Pray specifically, asking Him to be your strength where you feel weak. If you're facing a situation that feels like too much, try repeating, "God, I trust in Your strength, not my own." When we humble ourselves and ask for help, we invite God's limitless power into our lives.

Father, thank You for Your mighty power that is working in my life. I choose to put my trust in You, knowing that Your strength is greater than any challenge I face. Help me to stand firm, just like Joshua, and walk in faith, trusting that You will bring victory. I know You are fighting for me, and I declare that I am strong in You. In Jesus' name, Amen.

Encouragement

Remember, God's strength is always available, but it requires us to surrender our own efforts and rely on Him fully. When you feel at the end of your rope, that's exactly where His power shines the brightest. Trust that God's might is with you, surrounding you, lifting you up. You're not fighting this battle alone; you're clothed in the strength of the Almighty. Stand firm, knowing that with God's power, you're more than equipped for whatever comes your way.

Fear Not, God is With You

I want to tell you today, whatever you're facing, you are not alone. You might feel overwhelmed, maybe even scared, but God is saying to you, "Do not fear. I've got you. I'm right here, and I'm not letting go." What a powerful promise that is! He will strengthen you, He will help you, and He will uphold you, no matter how big the storm may seem. So take heart and step forward with courage, knowing that His unfailing love surrounds you and His mighty hand will see you through.

Let's look at the story of Elijah. He was a mighty prophet, a man of God who performed great miracles. He called down fire from heaven, defeated false prophets, and saw the power of God move in incredible ways. But even someone as strong as Elijah had moments of fear. After his great victory on Mount Carmel, Elijah was threatened by Queen Jezebel and, in fear for his life, fled into the wilderness. He was so overwhelmed and discouraged that he even prayed for God to take his life.

But here's the key—God didn't leave Elijah in his fear or despair. In that lonely, desperate moment, God came to Elijah and reassured him. He sent an angel to strengthen him, providing food and water for his journey. And then, in the stillness of a cave, Elijah heard God's gentle whisper. God wasn't done with him yet. He still had a purpose, and God reminded Elijah that he wasn't alone. In that moment, Elijah found the strength to carry on, because God was with him.

What are you carrying today that's filling you with fear? God says, "Fear not, for I am with you." You don't have to face it alone. Whether it's finances, health, relationships, or something else entirely, God's promise to you is clear—He will strengthen you, He will help you, and He will uphold you. Don't let fear take control. Surrender it to God and trust that He's walking through this with you, ready to lift you up.

Father, I come to You today feeling overwhelmed by the struggles I'm facing. But I thank You that I don't have to face them alone. Your word says that I don't have to fear because You are with me. You promise to strengthen me and uphold me with Your righteous hand. Today, I choose to trust You, to release my fears to You, and to walk in faith that You are working all things out for my good. In Jesus' name, Amen.

Encouragement

God's with you—right now. You don't need to have all the answers. His strength has your back. When fear tries to creep in, shut it down—because God's on your side, clearing the path and lifting you higher. Be bold and be confident, because He's making moves in your favor. You're never alone in this race. Trust Him, and watch how He turns fear into victory, every single time!

Called to Follow in His Steps

"To this you were called, because Christ suffered for you, leaving you an example, that you should follow in his steps."
~ 1 Peter 2:21 (NIV)

You are called to follow in the footsteps of Jesus. Not just in the easy moments, but especially when life gets tough. 1 Peter 2:21 says that Christ suffered for us, leaving us an example to follow. We aren't just called to walk a path of comfort, but to rise in faith even when the road ahead looks difficult. And here's the truth—you are equipped for that journey. You are called to something greater!

Think about Peter, the very author of this verse. Peter was bold, passionate, and devoted to Jesus. Yet, when the moment came for him to stand firm in his faith, he denied Christ three times. He experienced failure, disappointment, and shame. But here's the incredible part: Jesus didn't leave Peter in that place of failure. After His resurrection, Jesus called Peter again, restoring him and giving him a new mission. Despite Peter's weakness, God used him mightily to build the early church.

Peter's journey is a powerful reminder that even when we stumble, God's grace is greater. Jesus didn't avoid hardship, and He doesn't expect us to either. Instead, He empowers us to follow in His steps, trusting that every challenge we face is an opportunity for God's strength to be made perfect in our weakness. Peter's greatest victories came after his biggest failures—because he chose to get back up and follow Jesus again.

The challenges you face aren't there to break you—they are there to shape you into the person God has called you to be. When you walk in the steps of Jesus, you are never walking alone. His strength is in you, His peace is with you, and His victory is yours. You're not just enduring hardship, you're being prepared for a future beyond anything you can imagine.

Today, don't let past mistakes or current challenges hold you back. Follow Jesus, step by step, trusting that He's using every situation to mold you into the person He's called you to be. Remember how Peter was restored. God's grace is always there to lift you up, no matter how far you feel you've fallen. Keep walking. Jesus is your strength. Trust that God is working through every situation for your good. Lean into His promises and watch as every step taken in faith transforms challenges into stepping stones toward your divine destiny.

Father, thank You for the example of Jesus, who showed us how to endure hardship and keep moving forward. Just like Peter, I know I will have moments of weakness, but help me to rise again, trusting in Your strength. Lead me, step by step, as I follow in Your path, knowing that You are working all things for my good. In Jesus' name, Amen.

Encouragement

You are called to follow in the footsteps of greatness! Just like Joseph and Jesus, your journey may have struggles, but those struggles are part of your victory. Stand tall, stay faithful, and trust that God is working in you and through you. The best is yet to come, and as you follow Jesus, you are walking into a destiny filled with purpose, power, and victory! Keep going, because God's plan for your life is unstoppable!

The Mystery of Transformation

> *"Listen, I tell you a mystery:*
> *We will not all sleep, but we*
> *will all be changed."*
> 1 Corinthians 15:51 (NIV)

God is all about transformation. He doesn't just fix up the old; He makes all things new. The mystery of life in Christ is that we're not just waiting for some future change—we're living in it right now! When you're in Christ, you've already started the transformation process that culminates in the glorious moment when we'll be fully changed, fully alive, and fully like Him.

Think about Moses for a moment. He went from a prince of Egypt to a fugitive shepherd, broken and lost. Yet in his weakest moment, God called him to greatness. Through a burning bush, God didn't just send Moses to free Israel from slavery—He transformed him into a fearless leader. The man who doubted himself, who feared speaking, stood before Pharaoh and declared, "Let my people go!" Moses didn't rely on his own strength; he tapped into the supernatural power of God.

But this transformation isn't just about Moses—it's about you. The same God who empowered Moses is ready to do something even greater in us. This life is just the beginning. God's ultimate transformation will come when Jesus returns, and in the blink of an eye, we'll be changed forever. The story doesn't end here—your greatest transformation is yet to come!

This isn't just about waiting for what's next—it's about the here and now, about God's power transforming you today. Each day, you're not who you were before; you're becoming who you're meant to be. Just like Moses, who doubted his strength but trusted in God's promise, you too are under construction by the divine architect. God is actively working within you, reshaping your weaknesses into strengths, preparing you for feats greater than you've ever imagined. Step boldly into today, knowing that very challenge is part of God's masterpiece in the making—you're being crafted for greatness. And the journey? It's only part of the story. The real victory comes when this transformation reaches its peak—the moment Jesus returns. At that instant, the work inside you will be complete, and you will stand in the full glory planned for you. Every challenge and change today prepares you for that ultimate moment. So embrace the process, trust the progression, and know that every step is bringing you closer to where you are destined to be.

Father, thank You for the transformation You are working in me right now. I trust You to change me, from the inside out, and to make me more like Jesus every day. Help me to walk in faith, knowing that You are doing a mighty work in me. I look forward to the day when I will be fully changed and stand in Your presence. Until then, I trust Your process, and I surrender every part of my life to You. In Jesus' name, Amen.

Encouragement

You're already in the game of transformation. Don't let today's struggles or doubts make you forget the fire inside you. Just like Moses went from a runaway to a champion, you're being molded into something greater than you've ever dreamed. And here's the kicker—one day, in an instant, everything will shift, and you'll stand in full victory. Keep moving, keep believing, because God's promise is real. Every step, every obstacle—He's shaping you into something unstoppable.

Living Through Christ

"I have been crucified with Christ and I no longer live, but Christ lives in me. The life I now live in the body, I live by faith in the Son of God, who loved me and gave himself for me."
— Galatians 2:20 (NIV)

When we come to faith in Christ, something profound happens. We don't just adopt a new belief system—we experience a complete transformation. We no longer live for ourselves, but for Christ. The old life—our selfish ambitions, our past mistakes, and even our fears—dies, and in its place, Christ begins to live through us. It's a new identity, a new life empowered by the very Spirit of God.

Look at Paul—before his encounter with Jesus, he was Saul, a proud Pharisee, persecuting Christians with zeal. His life was all about legalism and self-righteousness. But on the road to Damascus, everything changed. Paul met the risen Christ, and in that moment, Paul wasn't driven by his own desires or ambitions—he was fully surrendered to Jesus. His old self was crucified, and Christ took over.

From that day forward, Paul became one of the most passionate apostles, traveling the world, preaching the gospel, enduring persecution and hardship—not by his own strength, but through the power of Christ living in him. Paul's story shows us what a life fully surrendered to Jesus can truly accomplish.

What about you? Have you come to that point of complete surrender, where you can say, "It's no longer I who live, but Christ who lives in me"? It's a powerful statement because it requires us to let go of control. It's no longer about what we want, but about what He wants to do through us. The good news is, when Christ is living in us, we're not left to our own strength. His Spirit guides us, empowers us, and enables us to live in ways we never thought possible.

No matter what you're facing today, remember this: Christ lives in you. You don't have to carry the weight of your burdens alone. You don't have to strive or struggle on your own. The same Christ who conquered death is the One living inside of you right now, giving you the strength, the peace, and the wisdom to walk through whatever challenges lie ahead.

Heavenly Father, thank You for the truth that Christ lives in me. Help me surrender more each day, trusting Your strength, guidance, and peace as I move forward. I'm not alone, and I live in the freedom Jesus gave me. Thank You for Your love and the gift of Your Son. In Jesus' name, Amen.

Encouragement

As you go about your day, let this truth sink deep into your heart: Christ is living in you. The old you is gone, and you now have the power of the risen Christ working in every area of your life. Whatever you face—be it trials, uncertainties, or even everyday decisions—know that you don't have to rely on your own strength. Surrender to Him, and watch how His grace, His power, and His presence guide you through. You're not just living for Christ; Christ is living through you—and that's where real victory is found.

Called to Something Greater

"Come, follow me," Jesus said, "and I will send you out to fish for people."

— *Matthew 4:19* (NIV)

Here is a perfect example about the power of calling—about stepping into something bigger than yourself. In Matthew 4:19, Jesus approaches two ordinary fishermen, Peter and Andrew, as they go about their daily work. With just a few simple words, He changes everything. He took them from their boats and nets and called them to a greater purpose—one that would impact the world for eternity.

Think about Peter, a man who spent his life fishing, providing for his family. It was a good and honest living, but Jesus saw more in Peter than Peter saw in himself. Jesus didn't just call Peter to leave his career—He called him to a new mission, to fish for souls and change lives. Peter could've stayed in his comfort zone, but he stepped out in faith and followed Jesus. That leap of faith in Peter's life became a testament to the power of God's call. He became a leader, a miracle worker, and the one who would help spread the gospel to the ends of the earth.

Just like Peter, God is calling *you* today. He's asking you to follow Him into something greater than what you can see right now. You might feel ordinary, or think your life is just "business as usual," but Jesus sees more in you than you see in yourself. He's calling you into a life of purpose, of influence, of impact. He's saying, "Come, follow me. I have a greater mission for you."

You may not feel ready. You might question if you're equipped, if you've got what it takes. But here's the truth: Jesus doesn't call the equipped—He *equips* the called. If He's calling you, He's already preparing everything you need to succeed. It's not about perfection—it's about showing up. Peter didn't have it all figured out, but he stepped up anyway. And look at the *incredible* things God did through him. Now, it's your turn. Step into the moment. Follow the call. Greatness is waiting!

Father, thank You for calling me to follow You. Help me to step out in faith, even when I feel unqualified or uncertain. I trust that You are leading me into a life of purpose and that You will equip me for the mission You've placed before me. Guide my steps, and use my life to impact others for Your glory. In Jesus' name, amen.

Encouragement

If you feel God calling you to something new, don't hold back—step out in faith. You may feel ordinary, but God has an extraordinary purpose for you. Don't settle for comfort when greatness is calling. Trust Him, just like Peter did, and watch your life transform. Whatever He's calling you to—whether reaching others, starting something new, or deepening your walk—know that He's with you every step. You're not alone. Following Jesus means stepping into a mission bigger than your fears, beyond your limits. Don't wait. The time is now. Follow Him and watch the extraordinary unfold.

Trusting Beyond What We See

"Now faith is the assurance of things hoped for, the conviction of things not seen."
~ Hebrews 11:1 (NIV)

This verse calls us to a bold and confident faith—a faith that doesn't rely on what's visible or certain but trusts in God's promises even when we can't see the outcome. In a world that constantly tells us to rely on facts, data, and tangible results, faith can feel like walking a road without a map, hoping for a destination we haven't yet glimpsed. But that's exactly what God calls us to: a life anchored not in what is seen, but in what He has promised. Living in faith means holding onto God's promises, even when the path ahead feels uncertain or the answers are hidden. It's choosing to believe that His plans are unfolding in perfect timing, even if we're still waiting. Faith doesn't deny reality; it transcends it, lifting our eyes beyond the challenges and allowing us to see with a heart grounded in hope. Each day of faith is a step closer to the life God has called us to, strengthening us to trust His character above our circumstances. In faith, we find the courage to walk forward, knowing that what we can't yet see, God is already preparing. Let your heart trust the journey, for with faith, every step brings you closer to His promise.

Living by faith isn't always easy, especially when circumstances around us suggest otherwise. It's natural to question, to feel moments of doubt, and to wish for visible proof. We're not perfect, and our understanding is limited, but that's where the power of faith shines. God invites us to place our hope and trust in Him, to see beyond the obstacles and believe that He is working in ways we may not yet understand. Faith is a daily choice to lean on God's word, even when the situation looks uncertain or when answers are delayed. It's a conviction that what He has promised will come to pass, even if we don't see it today. Faith reminds us that even in our uncertainty, God is unwavering and steadfast. It's the quiet strength that keeps us moving forward, knowing that our trust is in a God who never fails. Each day we choose faith, we're choosing to align our hearts with His plans, embracing the mystery of His perfect timing. And though we may not see the full picture, we can walk boldly, knowing that every step of faith draws us closer to the beauty He has prepared. Today, choose to exercise faith by trusting God with something that feels uncertain. Perhaps you're in a situation where you're seeking clarity or a breakthrough. Take a moment to pray, laying down your need for control and asking God to strengthen your faith. Let go of the pressure to see everything clearly right now, and choose to believe that God is working on your behalf. Trust that He holds your future, even when you can't see the full picture.

"Father, thank You for calling me to live by faith. Help me to trust You when things seem unclear and to find assurance in Your promises. Strengthen my faith and give me the courage to walk with confidence, knowing You are at work even when I can't see it. Let my life be a reflection of hope and trust in You. In Jesus' name, Amen."

Encouragement

Faith isn't about having every answer; it's about trust. God knows the path ahead, inviting you to lean into His promises and find rest in His love. Embrace the unknown—this is where He shapes you for something greater. Stand strong—God's plans are bigger than you can imagine.

Walking in Love

"Follow God's example, therefore, as dearly loved children and walk in the way of love, just as Christ loved us and gave himself up for us as a fragrant offering and sacrifice to God."
— Ephesians 5:1-2 (NIV)

I want to bring you into the heart of what it truly means to follow Christ. In Ephesians 5:1-2, the Apostle Paul calls us to the highest standard: to be imitators of God. This is not just an instruction—it is an invitation to live a life marked by love. And not just any kind of love, but the kind of love Christ showed when He gave Himself for us. It's sacrificial, intentional, and life-changing.

Look at Stephen—the first martyr and a powerful example of love in action. Even when surrounded by those who wanted to kill him, Stephen didn't fight back with hate. Instead, he followed Christ's example of sacrificial love, praying, "Lord, do not hold this sin against them." His love wasn't based on how he was treated; it reflected the love of Christ within him.
This is the kind of love Paul talks about in Ephesians 5: love that gives, sacrifices, and chooses grace over judgment. It's not easy, it often demands that we put aside our pride, our rights, and our comforts, but when we walk in it, we show the world the heart of God.

What would your life look like if you chose to walk in love, just as Christ did? Imagine the impact—on your family, your workplace, your community—if you became a reflection of God's love in every word, action, and choice. This love doesn't just change others; it transforms you. The more you love like Christ, the more you become like Him—and the more the world sees His beauty, grace, and truth.

Today, make a conscious decision to imitate God in the way you love others. When someone wrongs you, respond with grace. When someone is in need, offer your time and help. Look for opportunities to love sacrificially, knowing that your love reflects the very nature of God. At home: Love through serving your family in small ways, being patient, kind, and forgiving. At work: Be a light by encouraging those around you, going the extra mile, and showing respect to everyone. In your community: Seek out ways to give back, to listen, and to be there for those who need support.

Heavenly Father, thank You for Your incredible love that never fails. Help me to be an imitator of You, to walk in love as Christ did. Give me the strength to love sacrificially, to forgive quickly, and to show grace generously. Let my life be a reflection of Your heart, and may others see Your love through me. I ask this in Jesus' name, Amen.

Encouragement

You are dearly loved by God. When you walk in His love, you're never walking alone—you're moving in step with the heart of Christ. His love empowers you to rise above the noise, the pain, and the struggles of life. Just like Stephen, your love has the power to impact the world around you. So today, walk boldly in that love. Live in a way that reflects Christ's grace and mercy. When you do, you're not just living —you're transforming lives, including your own. Step into this calling with confidence, knowing that God's love is alive in you. Watch how it changes everything!

Boldness, Not Fear

"For God has not given us a spirit of fear, but of power and of love and of a sound mind."
– 2 Timothy 1:7 (NIV)

God has placed power inside of you! No matter what you're facing, no matter what fear tries to whisper in your ear, remember that fear is not from God. He's given you a spirit of boldness, a spirit of love, and a spirit of self-discipline. You are equipped for victory in every situation!

Let me share with you the story of Joshua. You see, after Moses passed away, Joshua was called to step up and lead the people of Israel into the Promised Land. Think about the weight of that responsibility! Joshua had been a faithful servant, but now he was being asked to lead the entire nation. The enemies in the land were fierce, the journey was daunting, and Joshua could have easily been overwhelmed by fear.

God told Joshua, "Be strong and courageous, for I am with you wherever you go." He wasn't alone—God had equipped him for the task ahead. Just like Joshua didn't have to rely on his own strength, neither do you. That same spirit of courage, love, and power is in you. Step into your calling with courage. You've got this! Fear can't stop you when God has already equipped you—trust Him, step forward in faith, and walk boldly knowing His promise is greater than any challenge.

What's the "Promised Land" God is calling you to today? A new opportunity, a bold dream, or breaking through a personal barrier? Whatever it is, don't let fear stand in your way. You're already equipped. Step into it—boldly, confidently, knowing that you've got everything you need to make it happen. This is your moment. Embrace it. Just like Joshua, you're not alone.

You have the spirit of power within you. You have the mind of Christ. You are loved beyond measure. Let go of fear, and walk in the strength that's already yours. The Promised Land isn't just a destination; it's a journey of faith, a place where you become who God created you to be. Every step forward, every risk you take, and every wall you break through is a step closer to that purpose. You were designed for more than playing it safe—you were made to conquer, to grow, and to thrive. Don't hold back; let the strength within you rise. Go after it with everything you've got.

Father, I thank You that You haven't given me a spirit of fear, but of power, love, and a sound mind. I choose today to walk in boldness, trusting that You have already equipped me for every challenge I face. Just as You were with Joshua, I know You are with me, leading me into the promises You have for my life. Help me to step out in faith and to trust Your strength within me. In Jesus' name, Amen.

Encouragement

Listen, God is with you every step of the way! When fear tries to rise up, remind yourself of the truth—you are not given a spirit of fear. God has already placed His power in you, His love around you, and His wisdom within you. When you trust in His promises, fear has no place. Walk in confidence today, knowing that like Joshua, you are stepping into your promised land with boldness, faith, and victory! This is your time—go forward with courage!

Held by Unfailing Love

"I have loved you with an everlasting love;
I have drawn you with unfailing
kindness."
- Jeremiah 31:3 (NIV)

These words are a beautiful reminder of God's unchanging, unconditional love for each of us. Imagine this: no matter what we do or how far we wander, God's kindness remains steady. In a world where love can feel conditional and people may abandon us if we don't meet their expectations, God's love stands apart. His love is unfailing—always reaching, always drawing us close, and never letting go.

Sometimes we may feel distant from God, perhaps burdened by past mistakes or struggling with self-worth. We may feel unworthy of love, convinced that we've strayed too far. But God's kindness is like a gentle hand, constantly reaching out, reminding them that His love never fades. Just as a parent lovingly waits with open arms for a wandering child to return, God is always ready to embrace us, just as we are. This is the power of His unfailing kindness; it doesn't depend on our worthiness but on His boundless compassion.

God's love is not a reward we earn but a gift He freely gives, rooted in a compassion that sees us through every high and low. It's a love that stands firm when we're weak, a love that whispers, "I am here" when we feel lost and alone. No past mistake, no present struggle, no future fear can separate us from His endless kindness. His love is woven into the fabric of our lives, guiding us, healing us, and offering a hope that goes beyond what the world can give. In His love, we find a grace that doesn't demand perfection but invites us to rest, knowing we are accepted fully. Step into that love—constant, unbreakable, and crafted just for you.

Today, let this truth sink in: God's love for you is everlasting, rooted in kindness that never wavers. If you're feeling disconnected or unworthy, remember that God's love isn't based on what you can give or accomplish; it's based on who He is. Make space in your heart to feel His kindness, to let go of guilt or shame, and to rest in the certainty that you are cherished. Take a few minutes in prayer, allowing God's presence to renew and uplift you, knowing that His love is strong enough to carry you through anything. God's love is a foundation that doesn't shift with life's storms; it's steady and unshakable, inviting you to find rest in Him. When we allow His kindness to touch the deepest parts of our hearts, healing begins, and strength flows where we once felt weak. Let go of the pressures of the world and simply lean into His embrace—He sees you, He values you, and He calls you His own. Trust in this love that surrounds you, and step forward with a confidence that only comes from knowing you're completely and eternally cherished.

"Father, thank You for Your everlasting love that never gives up on me. Help me to rest in Your unfailing kindness, to let go of any feelings of unworthiness, and to trust in Your heart for me. Remind me each day that Your love is constant, that it surrounds me, and that it's all I need. Draw me closer, and let my life reflect Your kindness. In Jesus' name, Amen."

Encouragement

You are held by a love that will not fail, a love that sees every part of you and still says, "You are mine." When you walk in this truth, you find freedom from the need for others' approval and strength to face life's challenges. God's kindness doesn't just surround you—it transforms you. Let His love be the foundation you stand on, the peace that fills your heart, and the light that guides you.

Living with Purpose

"You were bought at a price. Therefore honor God with your bodies."
— 1 Corinthians 6:20 (NIV)

In 1 Corinthians 6:20, Paul speaks to the profound value God places on each of us. He reminds us that we are not our own; we were bought at a price—the highest price. Imagine this in a modern context: think about how we treat something precious that we've invested heavily in, something we've worked hard to attain, whether it's a new car, a family heirloom, or something that holds deep sentimental value. We take care of it, treat it with respect, and make sure it remains in good condition. Now imagine that God Himself did this for you. He invested everything, paying with the life of His Son so that you could have eternal value and purpose. You are worth more to Him than you could ever imagine. God sees you as a masterpiece, deserving of honor, purpose, and unwavering love. Live each day with the knowledge that you are God's prized possession—step into the world with confidence, because you're valued beyond measure.

In this verse, Paul calls us to live in a way that reflects the worth God has placed on us. This means treating ourselves—our bodies, minds, and lives—with honor, integrity, and respect. It's about living intentionally, knowing we are created for more than mere survival. Instead of letting the world define who we are, we are called to align with God's purpose, making decisions that reflect His love and holiness. Living with this mindset isn't about perfection; it's about letting God's love transform how we see ourselves and how we walk through life. When we embrace this truth, we start to see every action as a chance to live out our God-given purpose. Step boldly, rise with unshakable confidence, and live as though every breath declares your worth—because God has spoken it, and nothing can stand in your way.

Today, take a moment to reflect on the immense value God places on you. Think about how He sees you—worth every sacrifice, every ounce of love, chosen and cherished. How are you treating yourself and the life He's given you? Are you speaking to yourself with kindness, making choices that honor your purpose, and living with the boldness that comes from knowing you're loved by the Almighty? Seek to honor Him not just in the big decisions but in the everyday moments, in your thoughts, words, and actions, letting each one be a reflection of His love. Remember, you're precious to Him, a masterpiece in His eyes, meant to live fully and fearlessly. Live like you know it—because to God, you're absolutely irresistible.

"Father, thank You for the price You paid for me and for seeing me as valuable. Help me to live in a way that honors You, to treat myself and my choices with the respect You intended. Guide me to see my worth in You and to walk boldly in Your purpose. In Jesus' name, Amen."

Encouragement

You are not ordinary; you are extraordinary in God's eyes. Live confidently, knowing that you were bought at a price and that your life has purpose, meaning, and value beyond measure. Embrace each moment with a heart full of grace, for you were crafted with intention, loved beyond comprehension. Let your spirit shine, for you are a masterpiece in the making, cherished by a love that knows no bounds. Step boldly into each day, for you carry within you a light that was designed to brighten the world and inspire those around you.

Living a life of faith means surrendering every plan, every fear, and every dream into hands greater than your own. It's the moment you realize that control is only an illusion—that, try as you might, there are limits to what you can handle on your own. Imagine holding onto a rope fraying at both ends, exhausted from trying to manage every outcome, every decision. Faith whispers, Let go.

This is the heart of true surrender: the willingness to release everything and say, "God, I trust You with it all." It's choosing to believe that He sees further, that He knows better, and that He loves deeper than we could ever understand. Giving up control isn't weakness; it's the strength to place everything in the hands of the One who controls it all. It's waking up each day with a peace that defies logic, knowing that whatever comes, you're guided by a God who holds every tomorrow.

This journey of faith is powerful—it transforms the way you live, releasing you from the burden of perfection and the fear of failure. In giving up control, you gain freedom, the kind of freedom that lets you dream bigger, risk more, and step out with courage. When you truly put everything in God's hands, you're not losing anything; you're gaining everything. Trust deeply, and let God's guidance empower you to shine without limits.

God's Commitment to You

"For the sake of his great name the Lord will not reject his people, because the Lord was pleased to make you his own."
— 1 Samuel 12:22 (NIV)

There's an incredible power in knowing that God chose you, not because you're perfect, but because He loves you. Imagine this: think of a coach who sticks with their team through every loss, every rough season, because they believe in them. God's commitment to you is infinitely greater than that. Even when you feel like you've messed up beyond repair or drifted too far, He's not giving up on you. His reputation, His glory, His very name is tied to your story. God is honored by calling you His own.

Think about what that means: the Creator of the universe, the King of all Kings, has chosen to call you His own. He knows your struggles, your insecurities, the ways you fall short—and He still says, "You are mine." There is no mistake, no season of doubt, no failure so great that it could make Him change His mind. His love is fiercely loyal, steadfast even when you're unsure or unsteady. God doesn't waver in His commitment to you, even when you're uncertain of your own worth. He's all-in, fully invested, and infinitely patient. So, when you feel like hiding or doubting if you're enough, remember that God sees you, loves you, and proudly claims you as His beloved. Hold your head high and walk with purpose, because the One who called you is faithful, and His commitment to you will never fade.

And here's the best part: God's commitment isn't just about accepting you; it's about empowering you. He's not content to leave you as you are; He's walking with you, shaping you, strengthening you, calling you higher. Every struggle, every challenge is an opportunity for Him to reveal His power through you. He doesn't just see who you are—He sees who you're becoming. So lean into His promises and step boldly into the life He's calling you to, knowing that His love, His grace, and His purpose are woven into every part of your journey.

Today, let God's unbreakable commitment fuel your confidence. When you feel discouraged or like you don't measure up, remind yourself that God chose you and remains committed to you. Reflect on the areas of your life where you feel rejected or overlooked, and remind yourself: the King of Kings calls you His own!

"Father, thank You for choosing me and calling me Yours. I am so grateful that Your love and commitment don't depend on my perfection. Help me to walk confidently, knowing I am accepted and loved by You. When I feel unworthy, remind me of Your faithfulness and renew my sense of purpose. Let Your commitment to me inspire a new boldness within me. I am Yours, now and forever. In Jesus' name, Amen."

Encouragement

Take heart! You are chosen, loved, and backed by the power of God Himself. No struggle, no setback, and no weakness can overshadow the purpose He has for you. Stand confidently in His love, knowing that He's not just with you—He's guiding, empowering, and cheering you on every step of the way. Embrace His promises, and let His strength lead you into the life He's crafted uniquely for you. You've got this because He's got you!

Stay Connected to the Source

I want to remind you of something powerful: you are connected to the ultimate Source—Jesus. In John 15:4, Jesus tells us to *remain in Him* because it's only when we are connected to Him that our lives will bear fruit. That means everything you need to thrive, to grow, to become who you were meant to be, comes from staying connected to Him. Staying connected to Jesus is where your strength, wisdom, and peace are continually renewed, empowering you to rise above life's challenges. When you remain in Him, you're not just existing—you're thriving, growing, and stepping boldly into the fullness of God's plan for you.

Let's take a moment to think about David. Before he became a king, before he was the giant-slayer, he was a shepherd. But what made David extraordinary wasn't his skill with a sling or his bravery in battle; it was his connection to God. David remained in the vine. Whether he was tending sheep in the fields or facing down Goliath, he knew his strength came from God. Every victory David experienced was because he stayed rooted in God's presence, trusting Him completely.

David didn't force his destiny—he let God grow it. The secret to a victorious life? Staying connected to the source. Stay rooted in Jesus, and watch as He shapes your future, fuels your power, and brings your dreams to life. Don't just survive—thrive! Stay connected, and let God do the rest. When you stay anchored in Him, every step forward is a step into purpose, passion, and true fulfillment.

Imagine this: a branch alone can't bear fruit—it thrives by staying connected to the vine. Just like that, when you stay connected to Jesus, His power, love, and peace naturally flow into your life, enriching every part. There's no need to force growth; just remain connected, and watch as your life blossoms effortlessly. Stay connected, stay empowered. Let go of the pressure to do it all yourself. Stay connected to the Source—Jesus. In your decisions, relationships, and work, let His strength and love guide you. When you lean into Him, you'll grow stronger, love deeper, and live bolder than you ever imagined. Make time to listen, stay close, and remember— you're never alone. His power is flowing through you, fueling your strength to overcome.

Father, thank You for being the source of everything I need. Help me to remain in You every day, trusting that when I stay connected to You, my life will bear fruit. I surrender my plans, my strength, and my fears to You. Empower me to walk in Your power and Your purpose. In Jesus' name, Amen.

Encouragement

You are connected to the true Vine, and in Him, you lack nothing. There's no need to force your way through life— stay rooted in Jesus, and He will provide all you need. When you remain in Him, the impossible becomes possible. Your greatest days are still ahead, so walk in faith and trust the process. Watch as God brings forth the fruit you were destined to bear. Keep moving forward, knowing you're never alone—you're connected to the One who makes all things possible!

Living in the Hope of Christ

"Though you have not seen Him, you love Him; and even though you do not see Him now, you believe in Him and are filled with an inexpressible and glorious joy."
~1 Peter 1:8 (NIV)

This verse calls us to a deeper kind of faith—one that's rooted not in what we can touch or see, but in the profound, unseen reality of Christ's presence in our lives. Faith in Jesus brings a joy that goes beyond our circumstances, a joy that doesn't fade even when life gets hard. This joy is not about pretending everything's perfect; it's about embracing the unshakable hope we have in Him. This kind of faith transforms how we live, filling us with a confidence that outlasts any storm. It's the assurance that, even in the unknown, we are held by a love that never fails. When life challenges us, this joy rises within, reminding us that we are connected to something greater, something eternal. It's a joy that fuels resilience, lifting us above the noise and grounding us in a peace the world can't give. In Christ, we're not just surviving—we're thriving, rooted in a promise that's bigger than our circumstances. Embrace this joy, let it lead you forward, and live boldly, knowing that with Him, your hope is unbreakable.

In a world that often tells us seeing is believing, it's easy to feel disconnected from God's promises when they aren't immediately visible. We may question, "How can I love or trust someone I haven't seen?" But Peter reminds us that true faith doesn't rely on sight—it relies on a relationship with Jesus that grows deeper with every step we take. Life brings challenges, moments of doubt, and times when we feel imperfect and inadequate. Yet it's in those very moments that God meets us, reminding us of His love and the joy found only in His presence. Faith is the whisper in the silence, the steady light in the unseen, guiding us to a love that transcends our understanding. In every step, even through shadows, God's presence is a quiet strength, a river of peace flowing within. When we surrender to this unseen grace, we find ourselves rooted in a joy that speaks directly to the soul, untouched by the world's fleeting noise. Today, embrace the joy of loving and believing in Christ, even when you don't have all the answers. When challenges arise, turn to Him in faith, allowing His love to fill the places of doubt and fear. Practice choosing joy over worry, trusting that He is near even when you can't see Him. Make it a daily habit to spend time with Jesus—whether through prayer, worship, or reflecting on His Word—and let that connection be your source of strength and peace.

"Father, thank You for the gift of joy that comes from knowing You. Help me to believe even when I can't see, to trust You fully, and to find strength in Your presence. Fill my heart with an inexpressible joy and teach me to walk confidently in the hope You provide. Let my faith be a light to others, pointing them to the joy only found in You. In Jesus' name, Amen."

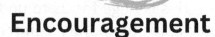

Encouragement

Remember, God's joy isn't bound by what you can see; it's anchored in His eternal promises. Even in trials, let the love of Christ fill you with an unexplainable joy that nothing can take away. Stand firm in your faith, knowing that your relationship with Him is real, powerful, and life-changing. Believe boldly, love deeply, and let your heart be filled with a joy that surpasses understanding. In the quiet surrender of trust, God's joy will be your strength, carrying you beyond every hardship. Let His love be the light in your heart, a gentle fire that warms even the coldest of days and brings hope to all who see it.

Your Advocate in Heaven

"Even now, my witness is in heaven; my advocate is on high. My intercessor is my friend as my eyes pour out tears to God; on behalf of a man, he pleads with God as one pleads for a friend."
— *Job 16:19-21* **(NIV)**

I want to dive deeper into a truth that is not only comforting but life-changing: *you are not alone in your struggles*. No matter how dark or overwhelming life becomes, you have someone far greater fighting for you—an Advocate in heaven, Jesus Christ Himself, who stands before God on your behalf. We find Job in the midst of his deepest suffering, feeling betrayed and abandoned by everyone around him. His health was shattered, his wealth lost, and his friends had turned their backs on him. Yet, in the middle of this overwhelming pain, Job declares something powerful: "Even now, my witness is in heaven; my advocate is on high."

This profound truth applies to you today. What Job is saying is that even though his earthly life was falling apart, there was still hope—because he knew God was watching, listening, and interceding for him. This is huge for us to understand. You see, Job wasn't just looking for temporary comfort; he was holding onto a higher truth. He knew that no matter how isolated he felt on earth, he wasn't abandoned in heaven. God was on his side, and an intercessor was pleading for him. Jesus Christ, who conquered death itself, is your Advocate. He stands before the Father, speaking on your behalf, turning your deepest struggles into victories. When you feel overlooked and misunderstood, remember—Jesus is actively pleading for you, transforming every tear into a testament of His enduring love and power.

Embrace this: You are not battling alone. Jesus, the ultimate Advocate, fights for you. Every challenge you face is met with His strength and advocacy. Stand strong, knowing that with Jesus on your side, victory isn't just possible—it's promised.

No matter how heavy your burdens feel, know that Jesus is with you, standing beside you every step of the way. He sees your pain, understands your struggles, and pleads for you before the Father with compassion and love. You're never abandoned—Jesus is actively working on your behalf, even in the moments when you can't see it. Just as He was faithful to Job, He is faithful to you, carrying you through every challenge with His unending grace.

Father, thank You for being my Advocate, for seeing my struggles, and for hearing my prayers. Help me to trust in Your presence and power, even when I can't see what You're doing. Thank You for interceding on my behalf, for fighting my battles, and for loving me through every challenge. I know I'm not alone because You are with me. In Jesus' name, Amen.

Encouragement

"For God so loved the world, He sent His only Son." Remember, even in your darkest times, Jesus is your ultimate supporter. He didn't endure the cross to leave you on your own. He's still fighting for you, believing in you—even when you doubt yourself. He is more than just your strength; He is your unwavering support, your foundation in every challenge. He's got you, always.

Living Faith That Moves Mountains

"And without faith it is impossible to please God, because anyone who comes to Him must believe that He exists and that He rewards those who earnestly seek Him."
— Hebrews 11:6 **(NIV)**

Faith often calls us to step into the unknown, trusting God's promises over our own understanding. Abraham was told, at 75 years old, to pack up everything and go to a land God hadn't even shown him yet. Imagine trying to explain that to your family: "We're moving, but I'm not exactly sure where." It sounds absurd! But Abraham didn't question God. He didn't ask for a roadmap or a set of directions; he just trusted that God was leading him. Living by faith requires stepping out, even when you don't see the full picture. Abraham didn't see the promise immediately. In fact, it took years for him to even begin seeing the results of his faith. But through it all, Abraham believed God was faithful.

Let's be real for a second. Sometimes having faith feels a bit like trying to assemble furniture without instructions, right? You've got all the parts laid out, you know it's supposed to work, but you have no idea how it all fits together. That's how life can feel when God asks us to trust Him. But here's the thing—God doesn't leave you hanging. He may not hand you the manual, but He's there every step of the way, guiding you through the process, one piece at a time.

Maybe God's calling you to take a step of faith—whether in your career, relationships, or ministry. Like Abraham, you may not see the full picture, and that's okay. God doesn't need you to know every detail; He just asks you to trust Him. Faith is the bridge between where you are and the promises God has ahead of you.

When you feel uncertain, take a step anyway. Faith isn't about seeing the whole staircase; it's about taking the first step, trusting God will show you the next. When you doubt, remember Abraham's story—his faith wasn't in the journey; it was in the God who called him. Focus on who God is, not on what you don't know. Trust in His power, step into the unknown with courage, and let your faith be the fuel that drives you forward. Embrace each challenge as an opportunity to witness His strength in action. Move boldly, inspired by faith, and watch as the impossible becomes your new reality.

Father, thank You for being faithful, even when I can't see the full picture. Help me to walk by faith like Abraham did, trusting that You are guiding my steps. When doubt creeps in, remind me of Your promises, and give me the courage to step out in faith, knowing You are with me. In Jesus' name, Amen.

Encouragement

Faith isn't about having all the answers—it's about trusting the One who does. Just like Abraham didn't need the full picture to take bold steps, you don't either. Faith moves mountains; it breaks barriers and opens doors that logic can't. Step up with boldness, courage, and relentless determination. Faith isn't just what you believe—it's what moves you forward. It's what unlocks God's favor and propels you toward greatness. This is your moment to rise, knowing that when you step out in faith, the rewards are already in motion. This is your moment. Let faith lead, and watch mountains move!

God Works It All for Good

"And we know that in all things God works for the good of those who love him, who have been called according to his purpose."
– Romans 8:28 (NIV)

God is always working for your good.! No matter what you're going through right now, no matter how tough or impossible it may seem, God's promise is clear—He's turning it around for your good. It's not just some things, not just the good things, but all things. When you live for Him, He's weaving everything together into a masterpiece, even when you can't see it yet.

Remember Joseph? He had dreams that God had given him—dreams of greatness, dreams of being used for a mighty purpose. But instead of seeing those dreams fulfilled right away, he was betrayed by his own brothers, sold into slavery, and thrown into prison for something he didn't even do. How easy would it have been for Joseph to give up, to think that his life had taken a turn that couldn't be fixed?

But here's the thing about Joseph: he never lost sight of who God was, even in the middle of the pit, even in prison. He held on to his faith, because he knew that God was still good, even when life wasn't. And you know what? God was working behind the scenes the whole time.

What looked like setbacks—slavery, false accusations, prison—were actually setups for something greater. Joseph went from the pit to the palace, from prisoner to the second-most powerful man in Egypt. And in the end, he saved his family and an entire nation from famine. What the enemy meant for evil, God turned for good!

What are you walking through today that doesn't make sense? Maybe it feels like everything is going wrong, like the dream you once had is slipping away. God is in the details. He's using everything—the highs, the lows, the disappointments, and even the pain—to bring about a greater good than you could ever imagine. Don't give up in the middle of the story, because God is still writing it. Just like with Joseph, He's setting you up for something bigger than you can see right now.

Father, thank You that no matter what I'm facing, I can trust You are working it all together for my good. Just like You did for Joseph, I believe You are turning every situation into a setup for something greater. Help me to see Your hand in the midst of my circumstances and give me the faith to keep moving forward, knowing that You are faithful to Your promises. In Jesus' name, Amen.

Encouragement

God's got you! He's in control, and He's not finished yet. Whatever is in front of you right now, God is using it for your good. Keep your eyes on Him, just like Joseph did. The pit doesn't define your story—God does. Trust in the process, because on the other side of this, there's a breakthrough waiting. So, don't lose heart. Keep trusting, keep pressing in, because He's working it all together for good!

Forgiveness That Frees

"Bear with each other and forgive one another if any of you has a grievance against someone. Forgive as the Lord forgave you."
– Colossians 3:13 (NIV)

I want to remind you today of the incredible power of forgiveness. You see, forgiveness is not just about letting someone else off the hook—it's about setting yourself free. When you forgive, you release the weight of bitterness, resentment, and anger that can weigh you down. And just as God has forgiven you, He's calling you to do the same for others. Forgiveness opens the door for you to move forward and experience the blessings God has in store for you.

Think about David and King Saul. David was a man after God's own heart, but Saul, consumed by jealousy, sought to destroy him. Saul tried to kill David multiple times, chasing him down with an army. David had every reason to hold a grudge, to become bitter and resentful. But what did David do? When given the opportunity to kill Saul and take revenge, David chose forgiveness. He said, "I will not touch the Lord's anointed" (1 Samuel 24:6).

David didn't let Saul's actions control him. He trusted that God would handle the situation, and he kept his heart pure. As a result, God elevated David to the throne and blessed him beyond measure. Forgiveness freed David to walk in his destiny, and it will do the same for you.

Maybe today, you're carrying the weight of a past hurt. Someone has wronged you, betrayed you, or spoken against you, and it feels like you have every right to hold on to that pain. Remember, forgiveness is not about the other person, it's about you. It's about releasing the hurt so that you can move forward into the fullness of God's plan for your life.

When you forgive, you're not saying that what the other person did was okay—you're simply choosing to rise above it. You're choosing to trust God with the outcome, knowing that He is your defender. Don't let a root of bitterness steal your joy or block your blessings. Forgive as the Lord has forgiven you, and watch as God opens doors of healing, peace, and favor in your life. Forgiveness isn't about forgetting—it's about freeing yourself from the weight of resentment and stepping into the fullness of God's peace. When you let go, you make space for God to work wonders in your heart, restoring what was lost and bringing beauty from brokenness. Embrace forgiveness, release the past, and step forward with power.

Father, thank You for the gift of forgiveness. Just as You have forgiven me, help me to forgive others. I don't want to carry the weight of bitterness or anger any longer. I release any hurt, any offense, and I trust You to handle every situation. I choose to walk in love, grace, and forgiveness, knowing that it will set me free to live in Your peace and purpose. In Jesus' name, Amen.

Encouragement

Listen, forgiveness is the key to your freedom. Just like David chose to let go of the hurt and forgive Saul, you can do the same. Don't let what someone else did hold you back from the blessings God has for you. Forgive them, release it, and trust that God is working on your behalf. When you walk in forgiveness, you're walking in victory. You're walking in the favor of God. So, let go of the past and step into the amazing future God has prepared for you! Forgiveness frees you to live the life God intended!

Be Doers of the Word

"Do not merely listen to the word, and so deceive yourselves. Do what it says."
— *James 1:22* (NIV)

Here is the simple but powerful truth: God's Word isn't just something we hear; it's something we LIVE. James 1:22 reminds us that if we only listen to God's Word without putting it into action, we're deceiving ourselves. We aren't called to be passive observers of the gospel—we're called to be doers, people who live out their faith boldly and with purpose.

Joshua didn't stop at God's promises—he could have easily rested on the assurance of victory, but that wasn't enough. God told him, "Be strong and courageous. Do not be afraid; I am with you wherever you go." But Joshua knew that hearing the promise wasn't where the battle was won. He had to take the next step: to act, to lead, and to trust God in real time. Marching around Jericho for seven days didn't make sense by human logic, but Joshua moved forward, believing that God's power would bring the walls down. His faith wasn't passive—it was active, and that's what led to victory. He didn't just hold onto God's promises—he lived them out.

Just like Joshua, God isn't asking you to just listen—He's calling you to move. Inspiration isn't enough. Real change happens when you act. You've already got everything you need to take that bold step of faith. The time isn't tomorrow, it's now. Step up, step out, and watch the impossible become possible!

God's Word is alive and powerful, but it only transforms when you put it into practice. What would happen if you didn't just listen but acted on everything God has spoken to you? When you live as a doer of the Word, you're aligning yourself with God's promises and stepping into a life of victory. Joshua didn't wait for a better time or an easier road—he acted on what God said, and the impossible became possible.

Don't just hear God's Word—act on it! Take what He's spoken to your heart and put it into motion. Whether it's forgiving someone, stepping out in faith, or sharing God's love with others, take action. Like Joshua, when you move in obedience, you'll see walls fall and breakthroughs come. Ask God what steps He's calling you to take today. Whether big or small, act on His Word, knowing He's with you. Trust that, God will make a way, even when the path ahead seems impossible.

Father, thank You for Your living Word that guides and empowers me. Help me not just to hear it but to live it out boldly. Give me the courage to step into obedience, even when it's hard or doesn't make sense. I trust that as I act on Your Word, You will bring walls down and open doors I never imagined. Thank You for being with me every step of the way. In Jesus' name, Amen.

Encouragement

You're not just a listener—you're a doer! Like Joshua, you're called to take action, step out in faith, and trust that when you move, God fights for you. The walls in front of you? No match for obedience. Step into your calling, act on God's Word, and watch the impossible unfold. Being a good listener isn't passive—it's an active, powerful choice to hear God's voice and let His guidance shape your steps. When you listen with intention, you're aligning yourself with His will, preparing to take action that's fueled by divine wisdom. Embrace the strength that comes from listening deeply, and step forward knowing every move is backed by God's promises. This is your moment—move boldly, break through, and claim your victory!

Grace for the Imperfect: A Love That Covers All

"For all have sinned and fall short of the glory of God."
~ Romans 3:23 (NIV)

Romans 3:23 tells us, "For all have sinned and fall short of the glory of God." This verse speaks to a profound truth: not one of us is perfect. In a world that often measures worth by success, beauty, or power, we can fall into the trap of thinking that being "good enough" will earn us God's love. But God's standard isn't human success or earthly achievements—it's holiness, a perfect goodness that none of us can reach on our own. Romans 3:23 reveals something crucial about our human condition—no matter how much we achieve, we're all in the same boat, imperfect and in need of God's grace. In our pursuit of perfection, we often overlook the fact that God's love isn't something we can earn through our own efforts; it's a gift freely given, a love that meets us exactly where we are. Our worth isn't found in worldly accomplishments or flawless exteriors, but in the deep, unchanging love that God has for each of us. So stop holding back—let God's love lift you higher, because every step forward begins with realizing you're enough in His eyes.

Think about social media today. We scroll through images of perfect lives, flawless families, and constant achievements, and it's easy to feel like we don't measure up. But Romans 3:23 is a reminder that behind every picture-perfect moment, every smile, and every filtered post, there is a human being who has their own struggles, mistakes, and imperfections. God sees us as we are, every flaw and failure, yet He calls us beloved, worthy of redemption through Christ, His response is one of grace. His love meets us right in our brokenness, and His mercy covers every shortfall.

Let this verse free you from the pressure of trying to be perfect. Instead of aiming to "earn" God's favor or approval, allow yourself to simply receive it. God's grace is a gift, not a reward. Today, try praying a simple prayer of surrender, offering your imperfect self to a perfect God. Let His love wash over your insecurities, your mistakes, and your fears. He doesn't need you to be perfect—He wants you just as you are. Trust that His grace fills every gap, turning your weaknesses into opportunities for His strength to shine. Embrace the freedom of being fully loved and accepted, not for what you've done, but simply for who you are in Him.

"Father, thank You for loving me as I am, with all my imperfections and failures. Teach me to stop striving for a perfection that only You possess. Help me to rest in Your grace and trust that I am enough because You are more than enough for me. Let my life reflect Your love and Your mercy, and let my imperfections be a testimony of Your amazing grace. In Jesus' name, Amen."

Encouragement

Remember, God doesn't expect us to live without mistakes. He knows our struggles and limitations and loves us through them. His grace is powerful enough to fill every gap, every shortcoming, every flaw. Rest in that truth and walk in the confidence that God's love is not dependent on your perfection.

God Can Do More Than You Imagine

"Now to Him who is able to do immeasurably more than all we ask or imagine, according to His power that is at work within us."
— Ephesians 3:20 (NIV)

Have you ever looked at your life and thought, "This is as good as it gets"? Or maybe you've found yourself thinking, "God might bless someone else that way, but not me." Ephesians 3:20 blows the lid off those kinds of thoughts. It says that God can do immeasurably more than all we can ask or even imagine! That means our biggest prayers, wildest dreams, and greatest hopes are small compared to what God is capable of doing. The good news? His power is already at work within you.

When God found Gideon, he was hiding in fear, overwhelmed by life's circumstances. The Midianites had oppressed Israel for years, and Gideon wasn't living the life of a mighty warrior —in fact, he felt anything but. His self-doubt and frustration were real. Gideon questioned God's plan, His own abilities, and even why things had gone so wrong for Israel. But God didn't choose Gideon for what he saw in himself. God chose him for what He was going to accomplish through him.

Now, think about your own life. How often do you feel like Gideon—hiding from challenges, weighed down by fear, feeling like you're the least likely candidate for the task ahead? Maybe you've questioned God's plan for you, wondering how you're supposed to step into something greater when you can barely handle what's in front of you. Just like Gideon, God isn't looking at what you think you can or can't do. He sees the incredible things He can accomplish through you, even when you feel unqualified. When God called Gideon to fight the Midianites, He didn't send him in with overwhelming numbers. Instead, He whittled Gideon's army from 32,000 to just 300 men. What looked impossible in human terms became the perfect setup for God to display His power. With just a small army, God delivered Israel and did immeasurably more than Gideon could have imagined. when you feel unqualified or overwhelmed, remember it's not about your strength, but what God can do through you. Like Gideon, trust Him to accomplish more than you think is possible.

Father, thank You that You can do more than I could ever ask or imagine. Help me to dream bigger, trust deeper, and walk in the confidence that Your power is at work in me. Like Gideon, give me the courage to step out in faith, even when things don't make sense, and to trust that You are able to do the impossible. Thank You for working behind the scenes, for seeing what I cannot see, and for guiding me into Your perfect will. In Jesus' name, Amen.

Encouragement

God's ability to bless, use, and guide you isn't limited by your past, resources, or doubts. His power is working in you, and He can do more than you've ever imagined. Like Gideon, you may feel inadequate, but God has already given you what you need. So, dream big, pray boldly, and trust that the best is yet to come. Your small efforts are enough because *He* is enough. Step out today, confident that God can turn your impossible into His possible. This is your moment—go for it!

Strengthened From Within

"I pray that out of His glorious riches He may strengthen you with power through His Spirit in your inner being."
— *Ephesians 3:16* (NIV)

We've all faced moments when we feel completely drained—physically, emotionally, and spiritually. Life can feel like a marathon, and sometimes we're running on empty. But Ephesians 3:16 reminds us that we don't have to rely on our own strength. God is ready and willing to strengthen us from the inside out, through His Spirit, providing exactly what we need to keep going. When we tap into His limitless power, we find a well of resilience and peace that carries us far beyond our own abilities.

Think about Elijah. Now, if there was ever a moment of total burnout, Elijah experienced it. He had just come off a major victory on Mount Carmel, where God showed up in an incredible way, defeating the prophets of Baal. You'd think Elijah would be riding high, right? Wrong. Not long after, he's running for his life from Queen Jezebel, and he's completely wiped out—mentally, physically, and spiritually. Elijah hits rock bottom. He even sits under a tree and asks God to take his life because he's done. Finished.

But here's the incredible part—God didn't scold Elijah for being weak. Instead, God provided for him, not just physically, but spiritually. An angel brought Elijah food and water, and then God told him to rest. Once Elijah had regained his strength, God met him in a gentle whisper, restoring him from the inside out. God didn't just give Elijah what he needed to survive; He gave him what he needed to thrive and finish the mission ahead. In that moment, God showed Elijah—and us—that He meets us in our lowest places, nurturing us back to purpose and reminding us that we are never alone in our journey.

How often do we find ourselves like Elijah? We pour ourselves out, we push through, but eventually, we hit a wall. We're exhausted, running on fumes, wondering if we can go any further. But the beauty of God's promise is that He offers us strength from His unlimited riches—not the kind of strength that fades, but the kind that empowers us to keep going, even when we feel like we have nothing left. In moments of exhaustion, Don't just push through. Take a moment to rest in God's presence and allow Him to fill you with His strength. Like Elijah, you may just need some spiritual "food" and rest. When you feel spiritually drained, Remember that God's Spirit within you is a source of power that never runs out. You can lean on Him when your strength is gone.

Father, thank You for strengthening me from the inside out through Your Spirit. When I feel drained, help me to rest in You and allow Your power to renew me. Just as You restored Elijah, I ask You to fill me with the strength I need to keep going and fulfill Your purpose for my life. In Jesus' name, Amen.

Encouragement

You don't have to run on empty—God's power is your fuel! Just like Elijah at his lowest, God meets you right where you are and fills you with unstoppable strength. He's not giving you a quick fix—He's offering you power straight from His limitless resources. It's time to rise up, recharge, and push beyond your limits. God's strength is all you need to keep moving forward. This isn't about just getting by—this is your moment to *thrive* and go further than you ever thought possible.

Lifted by Faith, Fueled by Hope

"But those who hope in the Lord will renew their strength. They will soar on wings like eagles; they will run and not grow weary, they will walk and not be faint."
— Isaiah 40:31 (NIV)

In a world that constantly demands more, it's easy to feel drained, like you're barely keeping up. Maybe you're exhausted from daily responsibilities, from the struggle to stay positive, or from carrying burdens you never expected. But Isaiah 40:31 gives us a powerful promise: those who put their hope in God won't just survive—they'll soar. God doesn't simply give us enough strength to get by; He offers us a divine power that lifts us above our struggles, giving us the endurance to keep going and the strength to rise above every challenge. His strength doesn't just match our needs; it exceeds them, taking us to places we never thought we could reach. When we rely on Him, every ounce of exhaustion transforms into a wellspring of energy, courage, and resilience. This isn't about surviving the day—this is about thriving with a power that sets you apart. With God's strength fueling you, you're not just facing the world; you're redefining what's possible.

This strength isn't about self-reliance or pushing harder. It's about surrender—letting God be the source of your renewal, your hope, and your fuel. When you feel worn down, place your trust in Him and watch as He fills you with energy, clarity, and resilience. In surrender, we find a strength that transcends limits, a power that isn't bound by exhaustion or circumstance. Instead of carrying life's weight on your own, you're invited to rest in God's unshakeable promise to carry you. With each step you take in trust, His strength becomes your strength, lifting you higher than you could ever go alone. Because with God as your source, you're not just moving forward—you're redefining what it means to truly live.

Today, take a few moments to release your burdens to God. Lay down every worry, every fear, and every doubt, trusting that His hands are big enough to hold it all. Ask Him to renew your strength, both mentally and physically, and to lift you to a place of hope and clarity. As you lean into His presence, let go of the weight you've been carrying and feel His peace fill the empty spaces. Know that you don't have to do it all—God's strength is ready and waiting to carry you farther than you ever thought possible. Take a deep breath, step forward, and embrace the unstoppable power that comes from walking side by side with Him. This is the kind of strength that sticks with you, the kind that lifts you up and never lets you down.

"Father, thank You for the promise of renewed strength. When I feel weary, remind me to hope in You and trust in Your power to lift me up. Help me soar above every struggle with the strength only You can give. In Jesus' name, Amen."

Encouragement

Isaiah 40:31 reminds us that those who place their hope in God will find a strength that doesn't run out, a power that lifts us up even in life's toughest moments. When you're feeling weary or like you're barely holding on, remember: God's strength is greater than any challenge you face. He promises to renew you, to give you endurance, and to help you rise above it all. You're not meant to just get by; you're meant to soar on wings like eagles, empowered by His love and lifted by His peace. Trust Him, lean in, and let His strength carry you —you're unstoppable with God by your side.

Mighty Warrior, God is With You

"When the angel of the Lord appeared to Gideon, he said, 'The Lord is with you, mighty warrior.'"
— Judges 6:12 (NIV)

In Judges 6:12, we find Gideon hiding in a winepress, threshing wheat out of fear of his enemies. He feels weak, overlooked, and unworthy. Yet God's message cuts through his insecurity like a lightning bolt: "The Lord is with you, mighty warrior." He calls Gideon mighty before he has even lifted a sword! God doesn't see Gideon as he is; He sees him as He designed him to be.

Think about those times you've felt small and defeated. Maybe it's at work, where you feel overlooked for that promotion, or in a personal struggle that seems impossible to overcome. We all have those "winepress" moments, don't we? Times when fear and doubt pin us down and keep us from stepping into who God created us to be. Sometimes it's the quiet voices of insecurity or comparison whispering, "You're not good enough." Other times, it's the weight of past failures, convincing you that you're stuck, destined to repeat the same mistakes. These are the moments when we feel hidden, just like Gideon, wondering if we even matter, wondering if God sees us and if He's truly with us. Yet, in the middle of that dark place, God speaks.

But here's the truth that can shake us free: God is with us! He sees the warrior inside you, even if all you see are weaknesses. When God calls you "mighty," it's not because of what you've done; it's because of who He is and what He's about to do through you. His presence changes everything.

Today, rise up. Step out of the shadows of doubt and fear. Own this truth: God is with you, and He calls you a mighty warrior! The challenge ahead? It's no match for His power within you. Believe it. Live it. And get ready—God's about to unleash wonders through you.

"Father, thank You for seeing me through eyes of strength and purpose, even when I feel weak. You call me a mighty warrior, and I want to live in that truth. Help me to see myself as You see me. Replace my doubts with Your courage, my fear with Your confidence. I invite You into every area of my life where I feel insecure or unworthy, knowing that with You, I am more than capable. Empower me to step out in faith, knowing that You are with me, guiding me, and strengthening me. I claim victory in every challenge before me, in Your mighty name. Amen."

Encouragement

Today, walk in the knowledge that God sees you as strong and capable, no matter how you may feel. Reflect on the areas of your life where you feel inadequate or fearful, and invite God into those spaces. Remind yourself that God's presence transforms fear into courage. Let His view of you —mighty warrior—reshape your own perspective. Approach your challenges not with doubt, but with the assurance that God is empowering you to overcome.

Standing Strong in God's Purpose

"Therefore, my dear brothers and sisters, stand firm. Let nothing move you. Always give yourselves fully to the work of the Lord, because you know that your labor in the Lord is not in vain."
— 1 Corinthians 15:58 (NIV)

There's a call in this verse that resonates with power and urgency. Paul is reminding us to stand firm, to let nothing sway us. In today's world, distractions, disappointments, and setbacks can make us question whether our efforts even matter. You might be working hard at your job, pouring into relationships, or serving in ministry, yet feel like your efforts are invisible or undervalued. But here's the truth: when you're working for the Lord, no action, no sacrifice, no ounce of effort goes unnoticed. God sees it all. Your labor is not in vain—it's building something eternal, something that lasts beyond the here and now.

Consider those moments that seem designed to make you throw in the towel—the times when exhaustion hits hard, when disappointment weighs heavy, or when the voices of doubt grow loud. Think about the obstacles that appear just when you're making progress, the setbacks that shake your confidence, and the fears that whisper, "Why keep trying?" Maybe it's the mountain of work that never seems to shrink, the relationships that feel one-sided, or the dreams that seem forever out of reach. These challenges push you to the edge, tempting you to walk away from the very purpose God placed in you. But it's in these moments, right at the breaking point, that God's strength rises up to carry you forward. These challenges may push you to the edge, but this is where champions are made—where God's power meets your persistence, lifting you higher than you ever thought possible. God's promise in 1 Corinthians 15:58 is that nothing done in His name is wasted. Every prayer, every act of kindness, every sacrifice made in love for God's kingdom counts. You are part of something far bigger than yourself, and God is using your faithfulness to make an impact that will outlast this life.

Today, commit to stand firm in whatever work God has called you to, whether it's serving your family, leading in ministry, or excelling at your job. When discouragement arises, remember that you're laboring for something eternal. Let God's purpose fuel your dedication, knowing that your work has lasting impact. So give it everything you've got—because with God on your side, you're building a legacy that nothing can tear down.

Father, thank You for giving my life and my work meaning beyond what I can see. Help me to stay steady and strong in the purpose You've given me. When I feel discouraged or weary, remind me that my efforts in Your name are never in vain. Strengthen my resolve, Lord, and let my heart be steadfast in Your work. In Jesus' name, Amen.

Encouragement

Your hard work matters to God. Even when the results aren't visible, He's using your faithfulness in ways you may not yet see. Stand firm, stay grounded, and let nothing shake you from your purpose in Him. Every step, every sacrifice, is building a story of impact and strength that heaven celebrates. So dig deep, push forward, and live boldly—your calling is unstoppable with God by your side.

God is Near the Brokenhearted

"The Lord is close to the brokenhearted and saves those who are crushed in spirit." —
Psalm 34:18 (NIV)

In Psalm 34:18, we're given one of the most beautiful promises of God's nearness, especially in times of heartache. Imagine it: when life's weight feels too heavy, when the pain seems too deep, and you feel utterly alone, God is right there, closer than your next breath. In a world where people can feel isolated even in a crowded room, God's presence is a promise that never fails. He's not just "around"; He's near, actively reaching out to heal, to comfort, and to restore.

Think about those moments in life when heartbreak hits hard. Maybe it's the loss of a relationship, a setback in your career, or the sting of rejection. Perhaps it's a season where nothing seems to be going right, and you feel crushed under the pressure. Just as a parent wraps their arms around a hurting child, God leans in closer to us during these times of brokenness. He doesn't require you to be strong first; He comes right where you are, offering the strength and comfort only He can give. There's power in knowing that God sees every tear, every hurt, and is ready to carry you through. So rise up with courage—because with God beside you, even your toughest moments are fuel for an unstoppable comeback.

When life knocks you down, when your spirit feels crushed—this is where God shows up strongest. Imagine the Creator of the universe, right there beside you, not as a distant observer but as your closest ally. He's not waiting for you to have it all together; He's stepping into your brokenness, into the mess, declaring, "You're not alone, and you're not finished." God doesn't stand by watching your struggle—He's the force that lifts you, the strength that fuels you, the hope that revives you. He's with you, and with Him, you're built to rise again. So stand up, lean in, and feel His power transforming your pain into purpose. This is your moment to discover that with God by your side, even heartbreak can't hold you back.

Today, if you're feeling broken or overwhelmed, remember that God's presence is closest to you in these moments. Allow yourself to lean into Him. Give Him your pain, your questions, and your fears. Don't try to handle it all on your own. Invite God into those hurting places and trust Him to lift you up. Let His nearness be your strength. You're not alone in the struggle—God is fighting for you, lifting you higher with every step. So stand tall, rise strong, and conquer—because with Him, you're built to overcome anything.

"Father, thank You for being close to me in my brokenness; remind me of Your love and healing. Help me trust that You're working all things for good, giving me strength and comfort in every struggle. Amen."

Encouragement

When you're at your weakest, God's love hits hardest. Your brokenness? It's not defeat—it's the opening for God's power to shine. He's not distant; He's right here, ready to unleash healing and hope. Lean in. Let Him take that pain and turn it into something unstoppable, something beautiful. This is where your comeback begins, and with God, nothing can hold you back.

God's goodness is limitless, flowing into the world through each of us, lighting up the darkest places and healing what is broken. Imagine the power of a world filled with hearts that mirror His love—a world where kindness replaces anger, where compassion bridges divides, and where forgiveness heals wounds. When we allow God to work through us, we become a beacon of His hope, a living testimony that love is stronger than hate, that light can conquer darkness.

To be an ambassador for Christ is to be the bridge, bringing heaven to earth in every act of love and grace we offer. Embrace this sacred role with humility and purpose, knowing that each moment you choose love over judgment, compassion over criticism, you draw others closer to God's heart. Go forth with courage, for you have been chosen to be His hands and feet, the voice of His peace, and the light of His love. In the smallest acts, be His love in action, lifting others as you walk, one step at a time, in the glow of His mercy and grace.

Seek Good, Seek God

"Seek good, not evil, that you may live. Then the Lord God Almighty will be with you, just as you say he is."
— *Amos 5:14* (NIV)

The call in Amos 5:14 is clear and powerful: "Seek good, not evil." It's an urgent reminder that God's presence is tied to our pursuit of what's right, true, and good. Imagine you're navigating the chaos of today's world—constant negativity in the news, voices shouting from every angle, and the weight of endless decisions. It's easy to feel pulled toward cynicism, anger, or hopelessness. But God invites us to respond differently. In the midst of darkness, we are called to actively seek good—to choose hope, to pursue kindness, and to live with integrity. When we do, we're not only transformed ourselves; we open the door for God to dwell with us in power and strength. So rise above the noise, choose the good, and let God's light shine through you.

Think about the influence your thoughts, words, and actions have, especially in times of stress. Seeking good means choosing God's way in even the smallest moments—when you turn away from gossip, when you choose encouragement over criticism, or when you hold onto hope instead of despair. These daily choices shape our hearts and align us with God's presence. He's ready to walk closely with those who intentionally seek Him, even when it's hard. It's not about perfection; it's about choosing to lean into His goodness when the world tempts us otherwise. Every choice for good is a victory, every act of kindness a step closer to purpose. Step up, stay strong, and let God's power flow through every decision you make.

Today, take intentional steps to seek out the good in every

situation, no matter how challenging it may seem. Challenge yourself to replace every negative thought with one of gratitude—see obstacles as opportunities and setbacks as setups for something greater. Speak words of kindness, even when it's easier to criticize, and let those words uplift both yourself and others around you. Find moments of quiet to reflect on God's goodness; let His peace ground you and renew your perspective. Every small choice, every intentional act, brings you closer to the God who promises to walk beside you, strengthening and guiding you through each step. As you seek Him in the little things, watch how His presence transforms the bigger picture.

"Father, thank You for the invitation to seek good and to find You in that pursuit. Help me to choose what is right, even when it's challenging, and to hold onto Your goodness in every moment. Let my actions reflect Your heart, and may Your presence be my guide and strength. Amen."

Encouragement

God sees every effort you make to seek His goodness, and He promises to be with you. When the world tries to pull you down, know that God's presence is your strength, lighting your path as you seek Him. Every step you take toward Him is a step into power, purpose, and peace that the world can't shake. Rise up, pursue the good, and let nothing hold you back— God is with you every step of the way!

Fearless in Faith

"Do not be afraid of those who kill the body but cannot kill the soul. Rather, be afraid of the One who can destroy both soul and body in hell."
— Matthew 10:28 (NIV)

In Matthew 10:28, Jesus speaks directly to the fears that can control us. It's natural to be afraid of physical threats or challenges—our instinct for self-preservation is strong. But Jesus reminds us here that there is a greater perspective we must keep: the health of our soul and our connection with God. Think about the pressures and fears we face daily—health issues, safety concerns, or societal expectations that press us to compromise our values. These are real concerns, but Jesus is calling us to a life of courageous faith, one that transcends worldly fears. He's saying that no earthly threat can ultimately harm who you are in Him. He wants you to fearlessly live out your faith, knowing that your soul is secure in His hands. With this perspective, we can stand firm, unshaken by the world's threats, because our ultimate strength comes from God. So rise with boldness, live with purpose, and know that your faith makes you unstoppable!

Imagine facing a health scare or the possibility of personal loss. These situations can make us feel vulnerable, but Jesus' words bring powerful assurance: nothing in this world has the power to touch the eternal life He has secured for you. Our bodies may be fragile, but our souls are protected by the One who conquered death itself. Jesus shifts our focus from temporary struggles to the everlasting peace and strength that comes from God. Instead of fearing what the world can do, we are invited to live fully and boldly in faith, trusting that God holds both our present and our eternity. So when life tries to shake you, remember you're standing on an unbreakable foundation. Face the world with unshakable confidence—your faith makes you stronger than any fear!

Today, commit to living with a fearless faith. Whenever worry about physical safety or worldly pressures starts to creep in, remember that your soul is secure with God. Trust Him with both your earthly concerns and your eternal security, and let His peace empower you to live courageously. Embrace each day as an opportunity to demonstrate the strength of your faith, showing the world how trust in God transforms fear into fortitude. Let your life be a testament to the power of divine assurance, inspiring others to seek the same fearless existence. Charge ahead, knowing that the battles you face are already won with God on your side—run your race with heart, and never back down.

"Father, thank You for the eternal security You've given me. Help me to rise above my fears and focus on Your promises instead of the threats around me. Give me the courage to live boldly and fearlessly, trusting that You hold my soul and my future. Strengthen my faith today, and let my confidence be in You alone. In Jesus' name, Amen."

Encouragement

Don't let fear of the temporary hold you back. God has already conquered the greatest threats, and He is with you every step of the way. Live boldly, knowing your soul is in the hands of the Almighty. Each day is a new chance to push past the limits fear tries to set, stepping into the freedom and courage God has given you. Face every challenge with the confidence that your strength comes from a power beyond this world. This is your moment—stand tall, rise up, and let nothing hold you down!

Stand Firm, God Fights for You

> "Moses answered the people, 'Do not be afraid. Stand firm and you will see the deliverance the Lord will bring you today. The Egyptians you see today you will never see again. The Lord will fight for you; you need only to be still.'"
> — Exodus 14:13-14 (NIV)

In Exodus 14, the Israelites were trapped between the Red Sea and the approaching Egyptian army. Fear and panic set in as they saw no way out. But Moses spoke a bold truth: "Stand firm... the Lord will fight for you." Imagine being in a situation where everything seems stacked against you, with no solution in sight. Maybe you're facing a health crisis, financial struggle, or an overwhelming emotional burden that feels impossible to escape. The instinct is to act, to fight in our own strength. But God calls us to a radical response: to be still and let Him fight for us. This isn't about giving up but about releasing control, trusting that God's deliverance is on the way.

This message is for those moments when we are stretched to our limits. When we try to make things happen on our own, we often end up exhausted and defeated. But Exodus 14 reminds us that God is a mighty defender, going ahead of us, working in ways we can't see. When we feel overwhelmed, we don't need to have every answer or control every outcome. God asks us to trust Him completely and promises to take care of the rest. Like the Israelites, we're called to stand firm in faith, expecting that God will make a way when there seems to be no way. He sees the path beyond our struggles, crafting miracles from what looks impossible. The battles we face aren't obstacles but opportunities to witness His power. So step back, take heart, and let God's power do what only He can—break through limits, exceed expectations, and bring victory to your story.

Today, take a moment to release your fears to God. Instead of scrambling for solutions, stand firm and be still, trusting that God is actively working on your behalf. Reflect on the areas where you need to let go and invite God to take over. When you surrender, you're not giving up—you're giving God permission to flood every corner of your life with His love and power. Watch as He takes what you release and turns it into something greater than you could ever imagine. Move forward with confidence, knowing that God is with you—and with Him by your side, there's nothing you can't conquer.

"Father, thank You for being my strength and my shield. In moments when I feel overwhelmed, remind me to be still and let You work on my behalf. Help me to stand firm in faith, trusting that You are fighting for me. Lead me through every challenge, and let Your power be seen in my life. In Jesus' name, Amen."

Encouragement

God is your defender, your deliverer, the one who stands between you and the storms of life with a strength that never wavers. In those moments when the weight of the world presses in, when it feels like you're up against impossible odds, remember: you don't have to face these battles on your own. You're not meant to carry every burden or solve every problem by sheer willpower. Stand firm, and let your heart rest in the knowledge that the same God who parted the Red Sea, who moved mountains for His people, is actively working on your behalf. His commitment to you is unbreakable, His power limitless. Trust Him, and watch as He brings a peace and purpose to your life that no storm can shake.

Strength in Every Setback

"We are hard pressed on every side, but not crushed; perplexed, but not in despair; persecuted, but not abandoned; struck down, but not destroyed."
— 2 Corinthians 4:8-9 **(NIV)**

Life has a way of pressing us from every angle, doesn't it? We face deadlines, disappointments, and doubts. Sometimes it feels like the walls are closing in, like every effort we make is met with resistance. Paul knew this feeling all too well, yet he stood firm, proclaiming that while we may be hard-pressed, we are not crushed. When Paul wrote these words, he wasn't talking from a place of comfort—he was in the trenches, facing hardship and persecution. Yet, he knew a deeper truth: that God's power shines brightest in our struggle. The very pressure we feel is where God's strength can pour through us, allowing us to endure beyond human capacity. So, when life pushes, stand stronger—God's power is breaking through, and nothing can hold you down. Each challenge is an opportunity to witness God turning pressure into purpose, refining us like gold through every trial.

Think about the last time life knocked you down. Maybe it was an unexpected job loss, a broken relationship, or a season of isolation. The world tells us to avoid pain at all costs, but Paul's words remind us that God is actively working in our lives through our challenges. We may feel struck down, but God says, "You're not destroyed." The same power that raised Christ from the dead is alive in us, empowering us to rise again and again God doesn't just rescue us from difficulty—He transforms us in it. Every setback, every bruise becomes an opportunity for His strength to be revealed, turning trials into testimonies. So stand up, shake off the dust, and show the world what God's power in you looks like.

Today, don't shy away from the pressures and pains. Instead, let them become reminders that God's strength is made perfect in your weakness. Trust that He's holding you up, even when you feel like you're falling apart. He's not just helping you endure—He's building resilience within you, turning each trial into a stepping stone. When you face those moments of doubt, look back and see how far He's already brought you. Every obstacle you overcome is proof that you're stronger than yesterday, more equipped for tomorrow. Embrace the journey, knowing God's power is making you unstoppable.

"Father, thank You for being my strength when I feel weak. Help me to embrace the trials I face, knowing that You are with me, pressing me forward. Transform my struggles into places where Your glory can be seen, and give me the courage to persevere, knowing that You are shaping me through every challenge. In Jesus' name, Amen."

Encouragement

When the world pushes you to the edge, God's power pulls you back. Your struggles don't define you—they refine you. Stand tall, knowing that God is with you, and let His strength shine through every crack and bruise. You're not just surviving—you're becoming unstoppable, fueled by a power greater than anything that comes against you. Embrace the journey, for with every challenge you overcome, you're sculpting a testimony of resilience and victory that echoes God's enduring faithfulness.

Letting God Shape Your Heart and Path

"For it is God who works in you to will and to act in order to fulfill his good purpose."
- Philippians 2:13 (NIV)

We often struggle to align our desires and actions with God's purpose for our lives. We may want to serve God, but fear, doubt, and sometimes just the noise of life seem to get in the way. Yet here's the good news: we don't have to carry the weight of fulfilling His purpose on our own. Paul reminds us that it is God Himself who is at work within us, shaping our desires and enabling us to accomplish His will. Isn't that powerful? He doesn't just call us; He equips and empowers us, so we're never left to face our mission alone.

God is like the master craftsman, fine-tuning our hearts to beat in rhythm with His. Every moment we surrender, He adds strength, courage, and a divine passion that takes us further than we ever imagined. When we feel weak, He steps in with power, turning our humble efforts into something extraordinary. So, no matter what lies ahead, remember: you are not walking alone—you're walking with the God of limitless possibilities. Stand tall, because when you align with His purpose, you become unstoppable, called, chosen, and empowered to leave a legacy that shines His glory!

Think of it this way: imagine you're an artist with a blank canvas but no inspiration, no brush, no paint. Then, God steps in, placing the tools in your hands, guiding each brushstroke, giving vision to your art. You don't need to come up with your life's purpose on your own or drum up the energy to do it. The Creator is at work within you, crafting something beautiful and meaningful, using your life as His canvas. All He asks is that you lean in, open your heart, and let Him lead.

Today, in every decision, invite God to guide your heart. Instead of struggling to figure out your purpose or trying to do it all in your own strength, surrender your will to Him. Ask God to give you a deeper passion for His plan and the strength to pursue it with all your heart. You'll be amazed at how He works in you and through you, making the impossible possible.

Trust that each step you take with Him is a step toward something extraordinary. As you let go of control, He opens doors you couldn't even imagine, replacing your worries with peace and your doubts with courage. Watch as He turns obstacles into stepping stones, using even the smallest of your efforts to create something profound. In His hands, your life becomes a masterpiece in progress, a journey of purpose, passion, and power—because when God is at the center, every moment holds the potential to change everything.

Father, thank You for working within me, shaping my heart to pursue Your will. I surrender my doubts and plans to You, trusting completely in Your strength to guide me with joy and confidence each day. In Jesus' name, Amen.

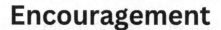

Encouragement

Know that God's work in you is constant and unrelenting. He doesn't start a project and leave it unfinished. God doesn't abandon you mid-journey. Whatever you're facing, trust that He is actively involved, stirring your heart, refining your will, and empowering your every step. When doubts creep in, remember: God is at work, transforming you for His glory. You are a masterpiece in progress, held in the hands of a Creator who sees the final, beautiful vision even when you cannot.

Building Others Up Through Truth and Love

"Instead, speaking the truth in love, we will grow to become in every respect the mature body of him who is the head, that is, Christ."
- Ephesians 4:15 (NIV)

In a world where truth often feels like a weapon, Ephesians 4:15 calls us to something radically different: to speak truth in love. Paul encourages believers not to shy away from the truth, nor to wield it harshly. Rather, our words should be guided by the heart of Christ, reflecting both His boldness and His boundless love. Truth without love can wound, but truth with love can heal and strengthen.

When we speak with the heart of Christ, our words have the power to lift burdens and open eyes, to bring both conviction and compassion. In a culture quick to criticize, we're called to build up, to reach people in ways that make them feel seen and valued. Each time we choose words that reflect Christ's love, we're setting a higher standard, showing that true strength comes from a tender heart. We're not just speaking to be heard but speaking to make a difference. So, go forward—speak truth with courage, with purpose, with love. Step into it with purpose.

Imagine a situation with a close friend or family member who needs guidance. The easy thing might be to avoid the difficult conversation to keep the peace. But what would Jesus do? He would approach with compassion, yet not back down from the truth. He'd speak with a love that's both fierce and gentle, aiming to restore, not just correct.

We're invited to follow in His footsteps, letting our words be rooted in grace and honesty, so they can truly heal. It takes courage to balance truth and love, but with every step, we're bringing the light of Christ into the lives of those around us. In choosing this path, we become agents of change, helping others see the beauty of growth. Embrace your voice, let it be a force for love, and watch as the world transforms—one word at a time.

Today, look for an opportunity to practice speaking the truth in love. Whether it's in a family discussion, at work, or with a friend, invite God to give you wisdom and grace in your words. Ask yourself, "How would Jesus say this?" Let His love guide your speech.

When you choose to speak with both honesty and compassion, you're creating space for growth and understanding to flourish. Each time you let love lead, you're planting seeds of healing that go far beyond the conversation. Embrace the strength in kindness, and let your words bring out the beauty in others.

Father, thank You for showing me the power of truth spoken in love. Help me to see every person through Your eyes and to speak with a heart full of compassion and honesty. May my words reflect Your grace, bringing healing and encouragement to those around me. Guide me to grow in Christlike maturity, using my voice for Your glory. In Jesus' name, Amen.

Encouragement

Remember, God is at work in you, giving you the courage to speak truth and the compassion to speak it well. Each time you choose love and truth together, you're becoming more like Christ, bringing His light into dark places and His peace into tense situations. You are equipped to be a voice of hope and a reflection of Jesus in every conversation.

Breaking Free from the World's Grip

"For everything in the world—the lust of the flesh, the lust of the eyes, and the pride of life—comes not from the Father but from the world."
~1 John 2:16 **(NIV)**

This verse speaks to three of the biggest traps we face: cravings of the body, desires for what we see, and the pride that sneaks in, telling us we can do life without God. John calls these things out, reminding us they don't come from God—they come from the world, a system that seeks to draw our hearts away from our true purpose and identity. The world around us is constantly pulling at our attention, convincing us that our worth lies in what we own, how we look, and what we achieve. It whispers that satisfaction is found in material success, that happiness is measured by the latest trends or status symbols. Every billboard, every social media scroll, every ad taps into our desire for more, subtly suggesting that we're not enough as we are. This is the world's influence—a relentless voice trying to replace God's truth with temporary pleasures that never fully satisfy. True success isn't measured by possessions or status, but by knowing that in God's eyes, you are already complete, already worthy, and already enough.

Think about it: every day we're bombarded by messages that say, "You need more to be happy." Ads, social media, and the world around us push the idea that satisfaction is just one more purchase, one more achievement, or one more experience away. But John is saying, "Don't fall for it." None of these things satisfy the soul. We chase them, thinking they'll fill us, but they leave us emptier than before. It's like drinking salt water when you're thirsty—it only makes the thirst worse. God's love is the only true source of satisfaction for the soul, filling the spaces that worldly things can't reach. His goodness is a well that never runs dry, a constant source of joy and peace that sustains us in ways material things never could. While the world offers fleeting pleasures, God offers a love that grounds us, a grace that renews us, and a purpose that fulfills us beyond any earthly success. When we understand that we are fully loved and accepted by Him, we find a peace that overpowers every empty promise the world throws at us. Resting in God's love frees us from the endless pursuit of "more" because, in Him, we already have everything we need. Today, ask yourself where you might be looking to the world for satisfaction instead of to God. Are there places where cravings or pride have quietly taken root? Be honest with yourself and with God. He doesn't expect you to be perfect, but He does call you to draw near to Him, letting go of the things that keep you from experiencing His fullness. Instead of seeking fulfillment in what the world offers, seek His presence, His purpose, and His peace. When we turn our eyes back to Him, He fills us with a joy and satisfaction that nothing in the world can give.

"Father, thank You for reminding me that true satisfaction comes from You alone. Help me to recognize and let go of the things in the world that try to pull me away from You. Teach me to seek Your presence above all else and to live with a heart fully devoted to You. Fill me with Your joy and peace that surpass all earthly desires. In Jesus' name, Amen."

Encouragement

You don't have to go through life striving for what the world says will make you happy. God's love is enough, His presence is enough, and in Him, you have everything you need. Trust that His way is better, and let Him redefine your desires. The world's promises are fleeting, but God's promises stand forever. You were made for more than this world's temporary pleasures—you were made for an eternal relationship with Him.

A Promise of Rescue and Redemption

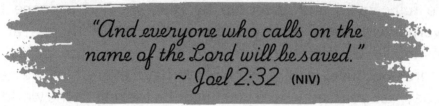

"And everyone who calls on the name of the Lord will be saved."
~ *Joel 2:32* **(NIV)**

In Joel 2:32, we find one of the most hopeful promises in Scripture: "And everyone who calls on the name of the Lord will be saved." Think about the power of that statement. Everyone—not the perfect, not the powerful, not the flawless—but everyone who reaches out to God, no matter where they are in life, can receive His saving grace. This verse doesn't put limitations or conditions on who can be saved. It's an invitation to the broken, the lost, and the weary, reminding us that no one is beyond the reach of God's love. God's grace isn't based on our performance; it's a gift that meets us exactly where we are, flaws and all. When we call on Him, His grace steps into the broken places, lifting us from despair and offering us new life. It's a love that sees beyond our failures, covering every weakness and mistake with mercy we could never earn. Grace takes us as we are but doesn't leave us there—it transforms us, giving us strength and hope that go beyond our human limits. This is the power of God's grace: it doesn't just reach us; it propels us forward, daring us to live fully, freely, and fearlessly.

In today's world, we often hear phrases like "You get what you deserve" or "You have to prove yourself." This mindset seeps into our thinking, and we might believe we need to be worthy of God's love. But Joel 2:32 breaks down that false belief: God's love and salvation aren't earned; they're given. Picture a lifeguard rushing to save someone drowning. The person struggling in the water doesn't need to prove they're worth saving—they simply need to call for help. God's rescue is just like that. No matter how "imperfect" we feel or how many times we've failed, when we call out to Him, He's right there, ready to save. God's grace dives in without hesitation, reaching us in our deepest struggles and darkest moments. We don't need to have it all together; we just need to call on Him, trusting that His love is stronger than our fears or failures. Just as a lifeguard pulls us to safety, God's grace empowers us to rise above the waves and live courageously—strong, free, and unafraid.

Today, let go of the idea that you need to "fix yourself" before coming to God. This verse encourages us to call on Him right in the middle of our struggles. Spend a few minutes in prayer, asking God to meet you where you are. Whether it's fear, doubt, or shame holding you back, know that God's heart is open and His arms are wide. Let Him in without hesitation, knowing He's already there, waiting to lift you up.

"Father, thank You for Your promise that all who call on You will be saved. I come with my imperfections, knowing You welcome me as I am. Help me release the pressure to be perfect and trust in Your grace. Remind me that Your love is greater than my failures and that I am safe in Your hands. In Jesus' name, Amen."

Encouragement

Remember, God's grace is for everyone. He's not waiting for perfection; He's looking for a willing heart. Calling on His name means surrendering the burden of self-sufficiency and choosing to trust in His strength instead of your own. You're never too far, too broken, or too flawed for His love. Embrace the truth that God's love doesn't require you to be perfect; it simply calls you to be His.

Finding Freedom Through Forgiveness

"Be kind and compassionate to one another, forgiving each other, just as in Christ God forgave you."
- Ephesians 4:32 (NIV)

In today's world, kindness and forgiveness can feel rare, especially when hurt and misunderstandings pile up. We hold onto grudges, bitterness, and even anger, thinking that holding back forgiveness somehow protects us. But Paul's words in Ephesians 4:32 call us to a higher standard. God's forgiveness is freely given, powerful, and life-changing. He isn't just calling us to let go of our hurt; He's calling us to model the forgiveness we've received from Christ—lavish, undeserved, and pure.

Imagine a coworker who's wronged you or a friend who's let you down. The easy response is to withdraw, to hold back kindness and guard your heart. But what would Jesus do? Jesus would choose to love, to forgive, to go beyond what feels fair. He would see the hurt but choose compassion. He knows that forgiveness is not weakness; it's the strongest act of love, one that frees both the giver and the receiver. God's forgiveness towards us isn't based on merit, and when we forgive others with that same mercy, we experience a freedom and peace that can only come from God.

Forgiveness has the power to unburden our souls, releasing the weight of resentment and bitterness that quietly erodes our peace. It's not merely an act of kindness to others; it's a gift to ourselves, a declaration of freedom from past pain. When we forgive, we step into a higher perspective, one that views others and ourselves through a lens of compassion and understanding. We create room for healing, for reconciliation, and for growth that can transform relationships and renew our hearts. Imagine a world where forgiveness is as essential as breathing—uncomplicated, accessible, and beautiful, an experience designed to change everything.

Today, take a step toward forgiveness and compassion. Whether by reaching out to someone who hurt you or letting go of bitterness in your heart, ask God to help you see them as He does. Let Christ's love be the lens through which you view them, choosing grace over judgment. When we open our hearts to compassion, we invite a peace that heals and restores. Imagine a world where forgiveness flows freely, where compassion is as close as the next heartbeat—effortless, pure, and transformative.

Father, thank You for the gift of Your forgiveness and the love You continually pour out on me. Help me to be kind and compassionate, to forgive as You have forgiven me. Let my heart be softened, my words be gentle, and my actions reflect Your love. Strengthen me to let go of any bitterness and to walk in the freedom You've given. In Jesus' name, Amen.

Encouragement

Remember, the kindness and compassion you show reflect God's character in a world that desperately needs it. When you forgive, you're releasing yourself from the chains of resentment and stepping into the peace of God's grace. The same power that freed you empowers you to set others free through forgiveness. Each act of grace you extend is a seed of healing, bringing light where there was once hurt. Let forgiveness be the gift that restores hope, because every step toward love makes the world a little bit better.

Walking Steadfast in Faith

"So then, just as you received Christ Jesus as Lord, continue to live your lives in him...overflowing with thankfulness."
-Colossians 2:6-7 **(NIV)**

This passage calls us to live deeply connected to Christ, rooted in Him like a strong, thriving tree drawing life from the soil. Just as we don't expect perfection from a young tree, God doesn't expect us to be perfect. Instead, He calls us to grow, to deepen, and to be transformed from the inside out by our connection to Him. Living like Christ means letting His love shape every part of who we are, choosing humility, kindness, and integrity as we walk through life. Just as a tree grows and flourishes from its roots, we are strengthened when we draw from the life and wisdom of Jesus, letting His Spirit nourish us daily. This is a call to not only know Him but to reflect Him, to let our actions, words, and thoughts align with His heart. Each step forward is a step of transformation, a move toward embodying His love more fully. Stand firm, grow deep, and let your life be a testament to the power of living like Christ—go all in, no turning back!

Think someone striving to find their footing in the chaos of daily life. Someone trying to balance relationships, work, and personal goals, but feels constantly pulled in every direction. Each disappointment shakes their confidence, and is often questioning if they're "good enough." In this verse we realize that God isn't looking for us to have everything figured out; He simply wants us to stay connected to Him, to keep growing, one step at a time. Instead of being perfect, we need to learn that our true strength comes from being "rooted and built up" in Christ—grounded in His love and strengthened by His truth.

Today, let this verse be a reminder to stay connected to Christ. Just like someone feeling uncertain, imperfect, or unsteady, we're called to deepen our roots in Him. When life pulls us in different directions, let's take time to pray, read His Word, and allow His strength to fill us. Instead of striving for perfection, let's focus on being anchored in Him. The deeper our roots grow, the more resilient we become, able to withstand life's storms and flourish in every season. Living rooted in Christ means drawing on His endless strength, not our own, so we can face each challenge with confidence. It's in our daily connection to Him that we find purpose, direction, and peace, no matter what comes our way. And just as trees grow stronger with every season, our faith grows deeper with every step we take in His presence. God's love holds us steady, and His promises give us a hope that never fades. Stand strong, stay rooted, and let your life bear the fruit of unshakable faith—this is where true growth begins.

"Father, thank You for being my foundation, for strengthening me even in my weaknesses. Help me to stay rooted in You, to grow in faith, and to walk in thankfulness. When I feel unsteady, remind me that You are my strength and that I don't have to be perfect. Keep me anchored in Your love, and let my life be a reflection of Your grace. In Jesus' name, Amen."

Encouragement

God is at work in you, shaping and building you up, even in your imperfection. Trust that He's using each moment to deepen your faith, to build you stronger than you were before. Don't let setbacks or failures define you; let your connection to Christ be the source of your confidence. As you walk with Him, you're growing into the person God created you to be, and that is a beautiful journey.

Boldly Embracing God's Grace

"Let us then approach God's throne of grace with confidence, so that we may receive mercy and find grace to help us in our time of need."
~Hebrews 4:16 (NIV)

This verse is an invitation to every believer, an invitation to come as we are—imperfect, broken, and often in need of help. It's a powerful reminder that God doesn't require perfection from us. Instead, He calls us to approach Him with confidence, knowing that His grace and mercy are there to catch us, sustain us, and empower us. This open invitation shatters the barriers of guilt and shame that often keep us distant from God. It reassures us that our flaws and failures are not obstacles but opportunities for His grace to manifest in our lives. By approaching His throne boldly, we acknowledge our dependence on Him and open ourselves to His transformative power. This confidence isn't born from our own abilities but from the unwavering faithfulness of God who meets us exactly where we are. Embracing this truth liberates us to live authentically, knowing that in His presence, we find the mercy and help we need for every moment. In the boundless embrace of His grace, we find that our brokenness is not a barrier, but a bridge leading us closer to His heart.

In a world that often values self-sufficiency and strength, it can be hard to admit our need for God. Society tells us to "keep it together" and to push through on our own, yet God invites us to do the opposite. He wants us to bring our burdens, our doubts, and our struggles to Him—not with hesitation or fear, but with a boldness born out of trust. God understands our weaknesses, and He offers a throne of grace, not judgment. He's waiting with open arms, ready to pour out His mercy and help us through every challenge we face. In a world that praises the unbreakable, God cherishes those who bring Him their fragile pieces. He sees the beauty in our surrender, the quiet strength in our reliance on Him. When we come to Him as we are—raw, real, unguarded—we find a love that fills every empty space and heals every hidden wound. Today, come before God without holding back. Bring your worries, guilt, and fears to Him, trusting not in your strength, but in His. Release the need for perfection, and rest in His grace—there you'll find the strength and peace your heart longs for.

"Father, thank You for the gift of Your grace. Help me to approach You boldly, trusting in Your mercy instead of my own strength. Let me find peace in Your presence and courage in Your love. Fill me with the confidence to come to You with all that I am, knowing that You are ready to help me in my time of need. In Jesus' name, Amen."

Encouragement

Remember, God's grace is not just for moments when we feel strong; it's for every moment, especially when we feel weak. He wants you to come with all that you are, fully aware of your flaws, and to step into His grace and mercy with confidence. God's love isn't something you have to earn—He's already offering it to you, abundantly and freely. So go boldly, trusting that His mercy is always greater than your mistakes, and His grace is enough to carry you through anything. Step into His embrace, for in His boundless love, even your deepest scars become a testament to His healing grace.

Made to Serve, Built to Love

"But made Himself nothing, taking the form of a servant, being born in the likeness of men."
~ Philippians 2:7 (NIV)

In Philippians 2:7, we encounter one of the most powerful demonstrations of humility the world has ever known. Paul tells us that Jesus, the very Son of God, made Himself nothing. Imagine that! The Creator of the universe didn't cling to His heavenly privileges or assert His divine rights. Instead, He took on flesh, choosing the life of a servant. He laid down His glory and put on humility to live among us, to experience our trials, our pains, and ultimately, to save us.

Making yourself "like nothing" means setting aside personal pride and status to embrace a life of service and humility. It's not about devaluing yourself; it's about lifting others up and choosing love over self-interest. Jesus showed us that true greatness isn't in exaltation, but in compassion and sacrifice, willingly lowering Himself to reach us at our level. This radical humility is a call to lead through love, to let go of ego and embrace purpose that serves a higher good. Imagine a life where selflessness is as natural as breathing—simple, powerful, transformative.

What does this look like today? Think about someone in a high position—maybe a CEO or a celebrated leader—who takes off the suit, rolls up their sleeves, and joins the team on the ground floor, listening, caring, and working beside them. It's a powerful thing to see authority and love in action, meeting people right where they are. This is what Jesus did for us! He traded His heavenly throne to step into our mess, showing us that real greatness is found in love, humility, and service. In a world driven by success metrics and titles, true leadership is defined by those willing to serve with empathy, setting aside rank to make a real difference.

What if we followed Jesus' example? Today, we're surrounded by messages that tell us to be "number one," to "stand out" and "assert ourselves." But Jesus calls us to a higher way: to "make ourselves nothing" and become servants. This isn't weakness—no, this is power wrapped in love. When we serve others, we demonstrate Christ's heart to the world. Maybe that means going out of your way to help a struggling coworker, listening patiently to someone who needs a friend, or simply doing an unnoticed act of kindness. True significance isn't found in elevating ourselves, but in lifting others up.

"Father, thank You for humbling Yourself to save me. Teach me to let go of pride and to follow Your example of true, selfless love. Help me to serve those around me with compassion and humility, not seeking praise but simply to reflect Your heart. Strengthen me to live out Your love in a way that others can see You through me. I want to walk as You walked, Lord, every day. In Jesus' name, Amen."

Encouragement

Jesus didn't come to lord over us; He came to love and serve us, and that same spirit lives within you! When you choose to humble yourself, you're not losing—you're reflecting the very nature of Christ. There is freedom and joy in laying down pride and choosing love. Let His example empower you to live boldly in love, shining brightly in a world that desperately needs to see real kindness. Embrace the beauty of a humble heart, where true strength glows from within and love becomes your lasting signature.

Grounded in Grace: Finding Strength Beyond Pride

"Though you soar like the eagle and make your nest among the stars, from there I will bring you down," declares the Lord.
~ Obadiah 1:4 **(NIV)**

In Obadiah 1:4, we see God's warning against pride, spoken to the people of Edom. They lived in high, seemingly unassailable mountain fortresses, and their pride convinced them they were untouchable. But God's message was clear: no matter how high they elevated themselves, they were not beyond His reach. This wasn't merely a warning for a people in ancient times; it's a call to each of us today. Pride can be deceptive, making us feel invincible and leading us to trust in our own strength or success instead of in God.

Think about a person today who has built a life of accomplishment—someone who seems to have it all: wealth, status, influence. We're told by society to "reach for the stars," but how often do we reach so high that we forget who gave us the wings to soar? This isn't to say success is wrong, but when pride blinds us to our need for God, we set ourselves up for a fall. Pride has a way of making us feel self-sufficient, convincing us that we have everything under control. It whispers that we don't need anyone else, that our accomplishments and status are enough to keep us secure. But in reality, pride acts like a shield, blocking us from fully seeing our deep need for God's wisdom, strength, and guidance. We become so focused on what we can do that we lose sight of the One who gives us life and purpose. Imagine a life where true strength comes from connection—reliable, unwavering, and always within reach. God's message to us here isn't about punishment; it's about realigning our hearts. When we soar on our own ego, we're bound to crash. But when we lift our hearts humbly to Him, God becomes our strength, our foundation.

This week, take time to examine your heart. Are there areas where pride has subtly crept in? Maybe it's in your work, your relationships, or even your faith. Acknowledge those areas before God, and ask Him to show you how to walk in humility. Humility isn't self-degradation; it's knowing our worth comes from Him, not from our accomplishments. Humility is recognizing that our value is rooted in God's love, not in what we achieve or how we measure up to others. It's about standing strong in who we are because we know who holds us up. Real strength isn't about standing alone—it's about knowing what drives you forward, step by step. When we live in this place, we're not only at peace, but we're open to God's guidance and ready to receive His blessings.

Father, I thank You for this reminder to walk humbly before You. Help me to recognize any pride in my heart and give me the courage to let it go. I want to live in Your strength, not in my own. Lift me up, Lord, and lead me to trust You more deeply, knowing that my true worth comes from You alone. In Jesus' name, Amen.

Encouragement

Remember, God isn't calling us to be lowly—He's calling us to be grounded in His love. Humility doesn't diminish us; it empowers us to grow in Him, giving us the strength to fly higher than we ever could on our own. When we depend on God, no storm can bring us down. With His love as our foundation, we rise with unshakable courage, ready to face any challenge and soar to new heights.

Living for an Audience of One

"I do not accept glory from human beings."
- John 5:41 (NIV)

In John 5:41, Jesus makes a bold declaration: "I do not accept glory from human beings." Jesus, the very Son of God, didn't come seeking validation from people. He didn't need human applause, praise, or recognition to know who He was. His purpose was rooted in God's will, and He lived with a confidence that transcended the need for human approval. This verse calls us to do the same: to live in a way that seeks to honor God above all else. God's love and glory are enough to satisfy every longing in our hearts, filling the deepest spaces that human praise could never reach. When we root ourselves in His love, we find a peace and security that can't be shaken by the shifting opinions of others. People's approval may feel good for a moment, but it fades, leaving us wanting more. But God's love is eternal, steadfast, and abundant—once we experience it, we realize there's nothing else that compares. Jesus shows us that when our identity is grounded in the Father's love, we can live freely, unburdened by the expectations and judgments of the world. Letting go of the need for human validation allows us to walk boldly, confident that we are fully known and fully loved by the One who created us.

In today's world, we're bombarded by messages that say we need to be "liked," followed, and praised. Social media, peer pressure, and even workplace culture can push us into a cycle of seeking approval from others. Think of Mike, a young man working hard to build his career. Every day, he checks his phone, hoping for positive feedback, wanting to be recognized by his colleagues and boss. But no matter how much praise he gets, he feels a constant emptiness. It's never enough because he's relying on human validation for his worth. When Mike reads John 5:41, it's a wake-up call—he realizes he's been living for an audience that will never fully satisfy him. He makes the choice to shift his focus, seeking God's approval first and letting that be the foundation of his identity. In today's world, we're bombarded by messages that say we need to be "liked," followed, and praised. Social media, peer pressure, and even workplace culture can push us into a cycle of seeking approval from others. Think of, a young man working hard to build his career. Every day, he checks his phone, hoping for positive feedback, wanting to be recognized by his colleagues and boss. But no matter how much praise he gets, he feels a constant emptiness. It's never enough because he's relying on human validation for his worth. In John 5:41, we realize it's a wake-up call—we realize we've been living for an audience that will never fully satisfy us. But when we turn our attention to God's love, we find a joy that doesn't depend on likes or recognition—a fulfillment that lasts. It's not about impressing the crowd; it's about living for the One who already sees our worth.

"Father, thank You for reminding me that Your approval is all I need. Help me release the desire for others' validation and focus on pleasing You alone. Root me in Your love and guide me in faith. In Jesus' name, Amen."

Encouragement

Remember, God's love and approval are constant. He doesn't need to be impressed; He simply asks for your heart. When you live for Him, you're free from the pressure to perform, to please, or to be something you're not. Let His love and purpose give you confidence, knowing that your life is held securely in His hands. Live boldly for Him, and experience the joy of living for an audience that will never let you down.

Overcoming Temptation with God's Power

"No temptation has overtaken you except what is common to mankind. And God is faithful; He will not let you be tempted beyond what you can bear. But when you are tempted, He will also provide a way out so that you can endure it."
-1 Corinthians 10:13-14 (NIV)

These verses carry a profound message of hope and strength: God doesn't leave us helpless in the face of temptation. Instead, He offers us His power and a way out, reminding us that we're not alone in our struggles. Even in our weakest moments, God's presence is unwavering, standing with us, ready to lift us up. When the pressure feels too heavy, He steps in, offering strength beyond our own, anchoring us in His unshakeable support. Just as a parent reaches out to steady a stumbling child, God's hand is always extended, guiding us, encouraging us to persevere. With Him by our side, we have everything we need to rise above any challenge, to face the storms, and to emerge stronger.

Life is full of moments that test our resolve. Maybe it's the pressure to fit in, the lure of quick fixes to our problems, or the quiet pull of distractions that lead us away from God's best. We all face temptations—moments when we feel our strength waning and wonder if we have what it takes to stand firm. The truth is, none of us are perfect. On our own, we're bound to stumble. But here's the good news: God knows our struggles, and His faithfulness meets us right there. He doesn't expect us to fight our battles alone. Instead, He promises a way of escape, a way to stand strong when we're feeling weak. In every challenge, God provides not only strength but also a path forward, lighting the way when everything else feels uncertain. He's there, equipping us with resilience to rise above and face every obstacle head-on. Push past the doubt, embrace His power, and stand unshaken—because with God, you're built to overcome.

Today, lean into this promise. If you're feeling overwhelmed by temptation or a struggle that seems too powerful, remember that God's strength is greater than anything you face. Take a moment to seek Him, to ask for the strength to walk the path He's laid out for you. Instead of relying on your own willpower, choose to trust in His faithfulness. Ask Him to open your eyes to the way out He's already provided and walk in that freedom, step by step. God's power is made perfect in your weakness, filling every gap with His unstoppable grace. So step forward boldly, let go of fear, and claim the victory that's already yours —run with faith, because nothing can hold you back.

"Father, thank You for being my strength in moments of weakness. Help me to see the way out You provide when temptation comes, and give me the courage to take it. Remind me that I'm not alone in this fight, that Your power is with me and that I can overcome because of Your faithfulness. Guide me to walk in Your ways and keep my heart focused on You. In Jesus' name, Amen."

Encouragement

God's faithfulness is your strength and your shield. He knows your weaknesses, but He also knows your potential. Don't let fear or shame keep you from reaching out to Him when temptation strikes. His grace is right there, offering you a way to rise above, to walk forward, and to live victoriously. With God by your side, you have the power to stand firm—stronger, freer, and more empowered than ever. Lean into His presence, knowing that every step you take in faith is backed by His unwavering support. Embrace the journey with confidence, for with God's strength in you, there's no limit to what you can overcome.

The goodness of Jesus is a wellspring that fills even the driest corners of our hearts. To walk closely with Him, to lean into His love, is to find a peace that the world cannot give nor take away. In His presence, the burdens we carry become lighter, and our souls find rest, not in the absence of hardship, but in the strength of His embrace. With Jesus, we are never truly alone; His love surrounds us, calms us, and gives us the courage to face each day with grace. Let His peace be your anchor, and His love your guiding light, for in Him, even the storm becomes a place of quiet trust.

When we root ourselves in Jesus, our hearts become steady, unshaken by the winds of worry and fear. He doesn't promise a life without trials, but He does promise to walk beside us through each one, filling us with a resilience that comes from His strength, not our own. The closer we draw to Him, the more we find our hearts aligned with His, our minds calmed by His wisdom, and our lives filled with purpose. In every moment of surrender, we learn that His grace is enough—that even in our weakness, He is our strength. Rest in His goodness, for He is the rock on which we stand, unmovable, faithful, and forever holding us close.

Choose Life: Embracing God's Path of Blessing

"This day I call the heavens and the earth as witnesses against you that I have set before you life and death, blessings and curses. Now choose life, so that you and your children may live."
~Deuteronomy 30:19 **(NIV)**

These words remind us of the power of our choices and the profound impact they have on our lives. God, in His love, offers us a path to blessing, peace, and purpose—but He doesn't force it on us. He simply invites us to choose. Each choice is a step toward the life God envisions for us—a life of purpose, strength, and unshakable peace. When we choose His path, we're not just making a decision; we're embracing a future shaped by His love and wisdom. This isn't about following rules; it's about unlocking the fullness of who we are in Him. Choose boldly, because every "yes" to God is a "yes" to a life that truly matters.

In today's world, we are constantly faced with decisions—some small, some life-changing—that shape our future. From the priorities we set to the voices we listen to, each choice either aligns us with God's will or pulls us away from it. We're not perfect; sometimes we stumble, sometimes we choose our own way over God's. Yet, in His grace, He continually calls us back, reminding us that we have the opportunity to choose His way each day. To choose life means to say "yes" to God's guidance, to lean into His love, and to trust that His ways lead to true fulfillment. Every choice becomes a whisper, a call to draw closer to the One who knows our hearts. When we choose His way, we step into a rhythm of grace that flows beyond our understanding, filling even our empty spaces with purpose. To choose God is to let go of our own shadows and walk fully in His light, embracing a love that transforms us from within. In each "yes" to Him, we find ourselves not just living, but truly alive, wrapped in the beauty of His endless grace.

Today, reflect on the choices before you. Are there areas in your life where you need to align more closely with God's will? Whether it's a decision in your relationships, your work, or your personal habits, invite God to guide you. Choosing life isn't always easy; it requires surrender and trust. But when we choose God's way, we're choosing a path filled with His blessings, His peace, and a purpose greater than ourselves. Each decision becomes a step toward the person you are meant to be, molded by the hands of a loving Creator. Walk courageously in His direction, for in every choice aligned with His will, you plant seeds of peace, purpose, and lasting joy.

"Father, thank You for the gift of choice and for the path of life You have set before me. Help me to choose Your way in every decision, to seek Your wisdom, and to follow Your guidance. When I stumble, draw me back to You and strengthen my heart to choose life each day. Fill me with Your love, and let my choices reflect my trust in You. In Jesus' name, Amen."

Encouragement

Remember, God doesn't expect perfection, but He does ask for a willing heart. He's patient, merciful, and always ready to help you realign with His path. Each day is a new opportunity to choose life, to embrace the blessings He has prepared for you. Trust in His goodness, knowing that with every choice toward Him, you're stepping into a life that overflows with His love and purpose. Stand firm, make the choice, and watch as He fills your life with meaning and joy.

Finding Strength in Trials

"Consider it pure joy, my brothers and sisters, whenever you face trials of many kinds, because you know that the testing of your faith produces perseverance."
~ James 1:2-3 (NIV)

At first glance, this can seem like an impossible task. How are we supposed to find joy in the midst of hardship? But James isn't asking us to ignore our pain or pretend we're fine. Instead, he's inviting us to see trials through a new lens, one where God is at work within us, refining and strengthening our faith.

Finding joy in hardship doesn't mean denying our struggles; it means trusting that God is using even our toughest moments to bring about something beautiful. It's the awareness that every challenge is an opportunity to grow deeper in faith, to become more resilient and more compassionate. This kind of joy is rooted in hope, not in the absence of pain, but in the presence of God's hand guiding us through it. When we shift our perspective, we begin to see trials not as setbacks but as stepping stones toward a stronger, more steadfast heart. Embrace the journey, knowing that each step forward is building a strength within you that nothing can shake.

Life often brings challenges we didn't ask for—unexpected difficulties, losses, and seasons of uncertainty. We may find ourselves questioning why we're facing such hardship and wonder if we're strong enough to handle it. But God knows our imperfections, our fears, and our weaknesses, and He isn't put off by them. He sees these trials as opportunities for growth, as moments where our faith can be tested and purified like gold in a fire. In the midst of trials, we learn to depend on God more deeply, letting go of our self-reliance and allowing His strength to carry us. It's in these difficult moments that our faith is stretched and deepened, producing the perseverance that only comes from walking through the fire with Him by our side. Every challenge becomes a refining moment, shaping you into the person God designed you to be. These trials are not meant to break you but to build resilience, courage, and an unshakable trust in Him. In the fire, you're transformed, gaining a depth of character and strength that only comes from walking through hardship. Embrace these moments, for they are forging a faith that is powerful, enduring, and uniquely yours—built to rise above. Today, instead of trying to escape or resent the challenges you face, try viewing them as opportunities for God to work in your life. Take a moment to acknowledge the difficulty, but also invite God into the struggle. Trust that He's using this season to strengthen your faith and to draw you closer to Him. When you feel the weight of the trial, remember that He is there to guide you, to lift you up, and to walk with you every step of the way. Embrace the process, knowing that God is shaping you for a greater purpose.

"Father, thank You for being with me in every season. Help me see trials as growth opportunities and find joy in Your presence. Strengthen my faith, teach me perseverance, and remind me that You're always working for my good. Let my life reflect Your love and resilience. In Jesus' name, Amen."

Encouragement

You don't have to be perfect to face life's challenges with courage. God's strength is made perfect in your weakness, and He promises to be with you in every trial. When you find joy in the midst of hardship, you're not ignoring the pain— you're choosing to trust that God is at work, using the struggle to shape you into someone stronger, more compassionate, and more resilient. Keep pressing on, because your endurance is producing a harvest of faith that will stand the test of time.

The Power of a Patient Heart

"My dear brothers and sisters, take note of this:
Everyone should be quick to listen, slow to speak,
and slow to become angry."
~ James 1:19 (NIV)

This verse speaks to the heart of how we should relate to others, calling us to approach each interaction with patience, humility, and grace. In a world that values quick responses and where conversations often feel like a race to be heard, James reminds us of a better way: a way that places love, understanding, and peace above the need to always have the last word. Our reactions to others reveal what's truly in our hearts. When we respond with patience and humility, we're demonstrating the love of Christ, inviting His peace into every situation. But when we rush to speak or let anger lead, we close the door to understanding and push others away from God's grace. In a culture that prizes being heard over listening, choosing restraint and empathy is a powerful testimony of our faith. James isn't just encouraging us to change our behavior; he's calling us to embody a deeper strength—the kind that stands firm, listens with intention, and speaks with purpose. Be relentless in your pursuit of grace-driven responses, because true strength is found in patience and power under control.

Imagine the impact of a world where people actually listened—where we put aside our need to defend, to justify, or to respond immediately, and simply focused on understanding each other. None of us are perfect, and we all know what it feels like to let anger get the best of us, to speak words we wish we could take back. But when we're quick to listen and slow to speak, we create room for God's grace to work through us. We make space for His peace to calm our spirits, for His wisdom to guide our words, and for His love to shape our responses. This verse challenges us to slow down, to let God's patience fill our hearts, and to approach others with the same grace He shows us.

Today, take a moment before responding to others—whether in a heated discussion, a simple conversation, or even in your thoughts. Let God's peace fill you, giving you the ability to listen fully and respond thoughtfully. Ask Him to help you be a vessel of patience and understanding, even in moments of frustration. As you practice this, you'll find that you're not only honoring God but also bringing His love into every interaction. In every conversation, you have the opportunity to reflect God's love and let His grace speak through you. Choosing patience over quick reactions allows His wisdom to shape your words, making your presence a calming force in a chaotic world. Each moment of restraint is a step toward embodying the peace He's placed within you. Let your words be a light—thoughtful, purposeful, and filled with grace.

"Father, thank You for the wisdom in Your Word. Help me to be quick to listen, slow to speak, and slow to anger. Teach me to reflect Your patience and grace in every interaction, allowing Your Spirit to guide my words and my heart. Fill me with the desire to understand others, to be a source of peace, and to bring Your love into each conversation. In Jesus' name, Amen."

Encouragement

God is shaping your heart to be more like His, teaching you to reflect His love through patience and understanding. When you choose to listen first, you're opening the door for God's Spirit to work in you and through you, transforming even the most challenging conversations. Trust that as you slow down, He will guide your words, soften your heart, and deepen your relationships. Let His love be the foundation of every conversation—speak less, listen more, and watch God's peace transform your life.

Choosing Grace Over Anger

"A person's wisdom yields patience; it is to one's glory to overlook an offense."
~Proverbs 19:11 (NIV)

This verse calls us to a life of patience and grace, reminding us that wisdom isn't just about knowledge but about how we respond to others, especially in moments of frustration or offense. In a world that's quick to react, quick to defend, and quick to criticize, God is inviting us to slow down, to be thoughtful, and to respond with His love instead of anger. This verse challenges us to rise above, to bring calm into the storm, and to choose peace when frustration tries to pull us down. True strength isn't in winning arguments or proving a point; it's in showing restraint, in choosing understanding over retaliation. In moments of tension, when emotions are high, we have the power to shift the atmosphere with a patient heart. Responding with grace is a choice—a choice that reflects God's love and leaves a lasting impact. It's about showing others that kindness is greater than anger, that patience has more power than pride. When you choose grace over frustration, you're not just reacting differently; you're setting a new standard.

Think about the everyday irritations and misunderstandings we face—moments that test our patience and push us toward reacting out of frustration. It could be a sharp word, a thoughtless action, or an unfair judgment. These moments tempt us to lash out or to hold onto resentment, yet Proverbs 19:11 reveals a higher way. God is calling us to overlook offenses, not because they don't hurt, but because forgiveness is a choice that strengthens our character and glorifies Him. By letting go, we're not only showing grace to others but allowing ourselves to live free from the chains of bitterness. Every time we choose forgiveness over anger, we're embracing a peace that lifts us above the pettiness of the moment. It's a powerful act of love, reminding us that holding on to grace is far greater than holding on to grudges. In letting go, we're not just moving past the hurt—we're creating space for joy and a life unburdened by resentment. Today, practice patience in your interactions. When you feel anger rising or an offense takes root, pause and remember this verse. Ask God for the wisdom to choose grace over retaliation. Let go of minor offenses, and let your response reflect the heart of Christ. Choosing patience and forgiveness doesn't make you weak; it reveals strength, allowing God's peace to reign in your life.

"Father, thank You for the wisdom found in Your Word. Help me to be patient and forgiving, choosing grace over anger in every situation. Teach me to reflect Your love, even when I feel hurt, and to find strength in overlooking offenses. Fill me with Your peace and remind me that true wisdom is shown through patience. In Jesus' name, Amen."

Encouragement

God knows we're not perfect, and He understands that patience is sometimes hard to find. But each time we choose to overlook an offense, we're embracing His wisdom and drawing closer to His heart. Remember, overlooking an offense isn't about ignoring justice—it's about finding freedom in grace and living a life that reflects God's love. Let patience be your strength, your guide, and your gift to those around you. In choosing patience, you're embracing a life where love speaks louder than anger and grace becomes your lasting legacy.

Guard Your Circle: The Power of Influence

"Do not be misled: 'Bad company corrupts good character.'"
~1 Corinthians 15:33 (NIV)

Paul's words are straightforward yet incredibly powerful. He's reminding us of the impact that our relationships and influences have on our lives. Whether we realize it or not, the people we spend time with shape our thoughts, values, and actions. We may think we're strong enough to resist negative influences, but over time, even a little compromise can shift our character. There's a popular saying, "You are the average of the five people you spend the most time with," and Paul's words echo this truth. Our closest relationships act like mirrors, reflecting back to us attitudes, behaviors, and mindsets that we often adopt without realizing it. When we're surrounded by people who are passionate about God, who encourage us to grow, and who stand by their values, it strengthens our own walk. But if we're constantly in the company of those who are indifferent to God's ways, it becomes easier to drift, to compromise, and to lose focus. The people around us can either lift us up or pull us down, shaping the course of our lives in profound ways. So choose your circle carefully, because who you surround yourself with has the power to either ignite your faith or slowly dim your light.

In today's world, "bad company" isn't limited to the people we see in person; it includes the media we consume, the voices we listen to, and the environments we place ourselves in. Social media, television, and even the casual conversations we engage in can either draw us closer to God's truth or pull us away. We're all imperfect, susceptible to the subtle tug of peer pressure or societal norms that go against the way of Christ. It can be as simple as laughing at a joke that doesn't align with our values, following trends that don't honor God, or tolerating attitudes that create division. The world may paint these things as harmless, but they're seeds that can take root if we're not careful. Every choice we make, from the voices we listen to, to the content we consume, shapes the soil of our hearts. Surround yourself with what uplifts and aligns with God's truth —let your life be filled with influences that help you grow stronger, bolder, and closer to His purpose.

Take a moment to assess your influences. Are there people, habits, or media that subtly pull you away from God's standards? Commit today to guard your heart by being intentional about your circle and the influences you allow. Choose to surround yourself with voices that uplift, encourage, and challenge you to grow in Christ. This doesn't mean isolating yourself from everyone, but it does mean prioritizing relationships and habits that bring you closer to God's purpose for you.

"Father, thank You for reminding me of the power of influence. Help me to recognize and remove any negative influences in my life that pull me away from You. Surround me with people who encourage me, inspire me, and draw me closer to You. Guide my steps, and fill me with the courage to live for Your purpose. In Jesus' name, Amen."

Encouragement

Remember, God has called you to a life of purpose and impact, but that calling requires intentionality. You're not alone in this journey—God's Spirit is with you, giving you the wisdom and strength to make choices that honor Him. When you surround yourself with positive influences, you'll find your faith strengthened, your joy deepened, and your purpose renewed. Stand firm, knowing that by guarding your heart, you're allowing God's goodness to flow through every area of your life.

The Power of Surrender

"Submit yourselves, then, to God. Resist the devil, and he will flee from you."
~ James 4:7 (NIV)

This verse calls us to a life of humility and surrender, and it's here that the true power lies. In a world that encourages self-reliance and independence, submitting to God might sound like weakness, but in His kingdom, surrender is strength. It's an invitation to stop fighting in our own power and to allow God's might to work in and through us. When we surrender to God, we become vessels for His power, allowing Him to accomplish what we could never achieve on our own. His strength flows through our weaknesses, turning our limitations into opportunities for His glory to shine. In our humility, He finds room to work miracles, to heal brokenness, and to bring peace in the midst of chaos. By letting go of control, we're not giving up; we're stepping into a partnership where God's limitless ability meets our willing hearts. This is the beauty of surrender —His power working through us, enabling us to live boldly, purposefully, and with a strength that transforms not only our lives but the lives of those around us.

We all know the struggle of dealing with temptations and personal battles—whether it's fear, anger, doubt, or the need for control. The truth is, none of us are perfect, and on our own, we're vulnerable to the devil's schemes. But James 4:7 reminds us that the key to overcoming isn't trying harder on our own; it's yielding to God. When we submit our hearts, desires, and weaknesses to Him, we open ourselves to His protection and guidance. It's only then that we gain the strength to resist the enemy effectively. By drawing near to God, we find a place of safety and power, a strength that doesn't waver even when the world around us does.

Today, choose to submit your life, your thoughts, and your struggles to God. Take a moment to lay down your burdens and admit that you need His help. Rather than relying on your own willpower, ask God to equip you with the strength to resist temptation and to stand firm against the enemy's lies. Remember that surrendering to God doesn't mean giving up control; it means placing yourself in the hands of the One who is fully in control. In surrendering, you're inviting God's wisdom to lead you, His peace to calm you, and His strength to empower you. Each time you let go, you're creating space for His power to flow through you, guiding your steps and renewing your spirit. Trust that in His hands, you're not only safe—you're unstoppable. Embrace this moment and live boldly, because with God directing your path, there's no limit to what you can achieve.

"Father, I come before You with a heart willing to submit. I lay down my worries, my fears, and my weaknesses, trusting that Your strength is more than enough for me. Help me to resist the enemy and to live in alignment with Your truth. Draw me closer to You, and let Your power guide my every step. In Jesus' name, Amen."

Encouragement

You don't have to face your battles alone. When you submit to God, you're aligning yourself with His power, and in that place, no enemy can stand against you. Every act of surrender is an invitation for God's strength to rise up within you, enabling you to live victoriously. Stand firm, resist the enemy, and watch him flee—because when you're surrendered to God, you're unstoppable.

Rising Above the Heat of Anger

"Do not be quickly provoked in your spirit, for anger resides in the lap of fools."
~ Ecclesiastes 7:9 (NIV)

This verse cuts straight to the heart, reminding us that while anger is a natural emotion, it's also a powerful force that can control us if we're not careful. Anger can feel justified, even righteous, when we're wronged or frustrated, but God calls us to something greater—self-control and patience. To let anger simmer unchecked is to let it take root in our hearts, eventually leading us down a path of bitterness and regret. This verse is a call to rise above, to harness our emotions rather than let them dictate our actions. Anger may come swiftly, but wisdom tells us to pause, to breathe, and to choose a response that reflects grace instead of wrath. Every moment we hold onto peace, we're choosing strength over impulse, creating a heart that is resilient and free. When we let go of anger, we're not just calming ourselves; we're opening the door to healing and forgiveness. God calls us to this higher path—not because it's easy, but because it leads to true freedom. Embrace patience, and let your heart be a beacon of peace in a world that often rushes to rage.

In today's world, where offenses come quickly and reactions are often immediate, it's easy to find ourselves consumed by anger. Social media, stressful workplaces, or tense relationships can all fuel emotions, making us feel that retaliation or harsh words are the answer. But Ecclesiastes 7:9 reveals a deeper wisdom: quick anger leads us nowhere but to foolishness. God isn't asking us to ignore injustice or pretend everything's fine—He's inviting us to handle our anger with wisdom, to breathe, and to let Him guide our responses. We're not perfect; we all have moments when anger gets the best of us. But each time we choose patience over pride, we grow a little closer to God's heart, reflecting His grace in a world that desperately needs it. In the quiet space between impulse and response lies the doorway to wisdom, where the heart learns to let go and the soul discovers the peace of divine grace. Today, practice patience when anger tries to take control. The next time something stirs frustration in you, pause and take a deep breath. Instead of reacting immediately, bring it to God in prayer. Ask Him to give you the strength to respond in love, even if it means saying nothing at all. Remember that your response can either escalate or de-escalate a situation. By choosing patience, you're choosing a path that honors God and brings peace. In that sacred pause, you reclaim the power to transform a moment of conflict into an act of compassion.

"Father, thank You for Your wisdom that teaches me to rise above anger. Help me to pause, to choose patience over pride, and to seek Your guidance in moments of frustration. Fill me with Your peace and remind me that true strength is found in self-control. Let my responses reflect Your love, even when I feel provoked. In Jesus' name, Amen."

Encouragement

God knows we're not perfect and that anger is a part of the human experience. But He's given us His Spirit to help us overcome it, to transform moments of frustration into opportunities for growth. When you choose to control your anger, you're choosing freedom from the trap of bitterness. Don't let anger hold you captive—let patience set you free, allowing God to work through you and bring light where there once was heat.

Finding Rest in His Presence

"Come to me, all you who are weary and burdened, and I will give you rest. Take my yoke upon you and learn from me, for I am gentle and humble in heart, and you will find rest for your souls."
~ *Matthew 11:28-29* **(NIV)**

These words are more than just an offer—they're a lifeline for the weary, a promise that true peace can only be found in Him. Jesus knows the weight of our burdens, the strain of carrying the pressures and expectations of life. He doesn't call us to ignore our responsibilities but to release the heaviness, to allow Him to share the load. In a world that often glorifies busyness and self-reliance, Jesus provides a counter-narrative of grace and rest. He understands our struggles intimately and invites us to exchange our burdens for His peace. This divine exchange isn't about weakness; it's about recognizing where our true strength comes from. It's a call to trust deeper, breathe easier, and walk lighter. Jesus is not a distant observer; He's an active participant in our lives, ready to bear our burdens and lead us into rest. Step into His strength, and watch as the impossible becomes manageable—because with Jesus, you're not just keeping up; you're soaring.

Think about the daily stresses and the constant demands on your time, energy, and attention. Life often feels like a race with no finish line, where exhaustion and anxiety can seem inevitable. We push ourselves, convinced that rest is a reward we must earn, a luxury for when everything is "handled." But Jesus challenges this mindset, inviting us to rest not as an escape, but as a necessity—an integral part of our relationship with Him. He offers us a new way of living, one where we don't have to do it all on our own but can rely on His strength and guidance. In Jesus, rest becomes a place of renewal rather than a fleeting break from the chaos. It's a state of surrender, where we allow His peace to refill what life has depleted and trust Him to handle what we cannot.

Today, take Jesus at His word. Whatever burdens you're carrying—worries about the future, financial stress, relationship struggles—bring them to Him. Trust that He's not only willing to help but fully able to lift what weighs you down. Surrendering doesn't mean ignoring your responsibilities; it means letting go of the need to control every outcome and trusting Him with the process. Spend time in prayer, laying down your burdens, and ask Him to fill you with His peace and strength. Let His presence be your anchor, steadying you in the midst of life's uncertainties. When you release control, you make room for God's power to work in ways you couldn't imagine. Embrace His peace, knowing that true strength isn't found in doing it all alone, but in leaning on the One who can carry you through every challenge.

"Father, thank You for the invitation to find rest in You. Teach me to let go of the need to carry everything on my own and to trust You with my burdens. Help me to take Your yoke upon me, to learn from Your gentleness, and to find true peace in Your presence. Strengthen me in my weakness and guide me in every step. In Jesus' name, Amen."

Encouragement

Remember, Jesus' yoke is easy and His burden is light. You don't have to navigate life alone or rely solely on your own strength. When you accept His invitation to rest, you're choosing to walk with the One who understands you fully and loves you deeply. Lean into His presence, and let His gentle, humble heart bring you the peace your soul craves. Trust Him completely, and experience the freedom of resting in His care.

Restoring with Grace: Lifting Others in Love

"Brothers and sisters, if someone is caught in a sin, you who live by the Spirit should restore that person gently. But watch yourselves, or you also may be tempted."
~ Galatians 6:1 (NIV)

Paul is calling us to a life of compassion and humility, a life where we are mindful of our own imperfections while reaching out to others in love. This verse isn't a call to judgment or condemnation but a call to restoration—a reminder that as followers of Christ, our purpose is to lift up, not tear down. Paul is challenging us to be people who breathe life and hope into those around us. It's a call to recognize the power we hold —not to crush, but to uplift, not to shame, but to restore. In a world quick to judge, we're called to be the hands that heal, showing the same grace that God extends to us every day. This is what it means to truly walk in the Spirit: to let our love be a light that pulls others out of darkness. Compassion isn't weakness; it's the courage to see brokenness and respond with mercy. When we approach others with humility, we honor God's heart, embodying His gentleness in a world that desperately needs it. Choose restoration over judgment—this is where real change happens, where lives are transformed, and where grace wins every time.

In our world, it's all too common to see people torn apart by criticism, especially in moments of weakness or failure. We live in a culture where judgment often takes center stage, and people's mistakes become headlines, social media posts, or whispered conversations. But Galatians 6:1 reminds us of a different approach, a higher calling. God asks us to step in with grace, to bring healing and restoration rather than shame. We are not called to ignore sin but to handle it with a spirit of gentleness, aware that we, too, have our own struggles and need for grace. Imagine a world where kindness prevails over criticism, where each stumble is met with an outstretched hand instead of a pointed finger. This is the vision Galatians 6:1 offers—a life where compassion heals and grace restores. Let's be the ones who choose love over judgment, creating a ripple of hope that lifts everyone higher. Today, let this verse challenge you to approach others with a heart of restoration. If you see someone struggling or caught in sin, pray for the wisdom and gentleness to help them without condemnation. Remember that none of us are perfect; we are all in need of God's grace. Seek to be a light, a source of encouragement, and an example of God's love. When we restore others with compassion, we are embodying the love of Christ and bringing hope to those who feel burdened by their mistakes.

"Father, thank You for the grace You show me each day. Help me to approach others with a spirit of gentleness and a heart of restoration. Remind me of my own need for grace so that I may extend it freely to those around me. Guide my words and actions, and let Your love flow through me as I seek to restore, uplift, and encourage others. In Jesus' name, Amen."

Encouragement

God calls you to be a vessel of His grace, lifting others rather than tearing them down. Don't let pride or judgment cloud your response to someone's struggle. Instead, be a reflection of His love and mercy. As you walk by the Spirit, allow Him to lead you in gentleness, knowing that the same grace God extended to you is what you are called to extend to others. Restoring others is an act of worship, a way of saying, "Lord, let Your love flow through me." In every act of compassion, you become a beacon of God's kindness, showing others that His love is boundless and His mercy never fails.

With God, the Impossible Becomes Possible

"With man this is impossible, but not with God; all things are possible with God."
~Mark 10:27 (NIV)

In a world that constantly reminds us of our limitations, this verse invites us to see beyond what we think is achievable. Jesus is telling us that while there are many things we can't do in our own strength, nothing is outside of God's ability. It's a call to look past human restrictions and rely fully on His limitless power. This verse challenges us to redefine what's possible, to lift our gaze from earthly boundaries to divine potential. God's power is infinite, unshaken by circumstances, unfazed by obstacles, and unlimited by human weakness. When we invite Him into our challenges, we're not just hoping for change; we're stepping into a reality where miracles can happen. Imagine the freedom of knowing that no setback, no failure, no obstacle can stop what God has purposed. Faith in His power gives us the courage to dream bigger, believe deeper, and walk boldly into the unknown. When we rely on His strength, the impossible becomes a canvas for His greatness. Dare to trust Him, and watch as He takes you further than you ever imagined.

We all face situations that seem insurmountable. Maybe it's a challenge at work, a relationship that feels too broken to mend, or a goal that feels completely out of reach. In these moments, it's easy to feel discouraged, to wonder if we're strong enough, smart enough, or good enough. But Jesus' words are a reminder that we don't have to be perfect, and we don't have to have it all figured out. God's power is made perfect in our weakness, and it's in our hardest battles that He shows up in ways we could never imagine. When we reach the end of our strength, that's where God's strength begins. In those moments of doubt and struggle, He steps in, turning our obstacles into opportunities for His grace to shine. We don't have to carry the weight alone—His love lifts us, His wisdom guides us, and His strength empowers us. Embrace the journey, knowing that with God by your side, even the toughest battles can lead to the most beautiful victories. Today, bring your "impossible" situations to God. Whatever has been weighing you down—whatever feels beyond your reach—place it in His hands. Ask Him to show His strength in the areas where you feel weak, to work miracles where you see no way forward. Trusting God with the impossible doesn't mean you sit back and do nothing; it means you step forward in faith, knowing that He's walking with you, opening doors, and moving mountains in His perfect timing.

"Father, thank You for reminding me that nothing is impossible with You. Help me release my doubts, trust Your power over my own, and strengthen my faith. Open my eyes to see Your work, and fill me with confidence, knowing You are with me. In Jesus' name, Amen."

Encouragement

Remember, God's power is not limited by human constraints. He specializes in doing the impossible, and He delights in revealing His glory through your faith. Let His words sink into your heart: *With God, all things are possible.* You don't need to have all the answers, just the courage to trust Him. Dare to believe that the God who created the universe is also deeply invested in every detail of your life—ready to turn obstacles into opportunities, fears into faith, and impossibilities into testimonies.

Unleashing God's Power Through Prayer

"After they prayed, the place where they were meeting was shaken. And they were all filled with the Holy Spirit and spoke the word of God boldly."
~ Acts 4:31 (NIV)

This verse captures a powerful moment in the early church—a moment where ordinary believers, in the face of threats and opposition, experienced an extraordinary move of God. They didn't rely on their own strength or eloquence. Instead, they prayed, sought God with all their hearts, and the Holy Spirit filled them with boldness. This was a courage not born of human confidence, but of divine empowerment. In that moment, they were completely consumed by the Holy Spirit, ignited with a passion that surpassed any earthly fear. The Spirit filled every corner of their hearts, pushing out hesitation and replacing it with an unshakable resolve to carry out God's will. It was a fire that couldn't be extinguished by threats or challenges—a relentless courage that came from knowing they were part of something far greater than themselves. When we are consumed by the Holy Spirit, we become vessels of His power, walking in a confidence that defies logic and radiates His love. This divine boldness transforms us, allowing us to step into places we never thought possible, to speak words we didn't think we had, and to impact lives with a strength that comes only from God.

In today's world, it's easy to feel intimidated, to shrink back from sharing our faith or standing firm in God's truth. The challenges we face—whether in workplaces, communities, or within ourselves—can make us feel inadequate or unprepared. None of us are perfect; we all have moments of fear and doubt. But just as in the early church, God invites us to lean into Him through prayer, asking for His Spirit to give us the boldness we can't muster on our own. When we surrender our weaknesses, the Holy Spirit steps in, filling us with a confidence that transforms our lives and empowers us to make an impact. In the quiet surrender of our fears, God breathes courage into our souls, giving us strength beyond what we can see or feel. When we open ourselves fully to His Spirit, we become instruments of His love, carrying His light into the darkest corners with a gentle, unyielding grace. Today, invite God's Spirit into your life with intentional, heartfelt prayer. Ask Him for the courage to stand firm in your faith, to speak truth with love, and to live out His purpose boldly. Trust that God will meet you there, equipping you to face challenges with strength beyond your own. When you feel hesitant or unsure, remember that the Spirit within you is greater than any fear or opposition. Let prayer be your foundation, knowing that through it, God can shake the ground of your circumstances and fill you with unshakable boldness.

"Father, thank You for the gift of Your Spirit and the boldness that comes through prayer. Fill me with Your power, and remove every doubt and fear within me. Strengthen my heart, that I may speak Your truth boldly and live out Your purpose confidently. Shake the places in my life that need Your touch, and let me walk in the assurance that You are with me. In Jesus' name, Amen."

Encouragement

You're called to live with power, love, and clarity—not fear. Let the Holy Spirit fill you, pushing past doubts and igniting courage. Step boldly into His purpose, unstoppable and empowered to make a difference.

Ambassadors of Christ:
Living as His Messengers of Reconciliation

"We are therefore Christ's ambassadors, as though God were making His appeal through us. We implore you on Christ's behalf: Be reconciled to God."
~2 Corinthians 5:20 (NIV)

This verse is both a calling and a reminder. As followers of Christ, we are not just recipients of His love and grace; we are representatives of it. God has entrusted us to carry His message of reconciliation to a world that is hurting and in need of hope. Our lives, our actions, our words—these are the instruments God uses to reach others. It's as though He is speaking through us, drawing people closer to His heart. Embrace this responsibility with unwavering determination, knowing that each moment you reflect God's love, you are building a bridge between heaven and earth. Stand firm in your purpose, for you have within you the power to inspire change, uplift spirits, and lead others toward the light of His grace. Carry His love like a flame in the darkness, letting its warmth reach those who feel forgotten and lost. Be the gentle hands of compassion, lifting others with a kindness that speaks of God's unending mercy and grace.

In today's world, it's easy to feel overwhelmed by division, anger, and brokenness. We see it in our communities, our workplaces, even in our own relationships. We're not perfect; we stumble, we make mistakes, and sometimes we fail to reflect God's love as we should. But God doesn't call us to be flawless; He calls us to be faithful. Being an ambassador for Christ means embracing His grace, walking in humility, and letting His love be our guide. Through His Spirit, we can extend forgiveness, offer compassion, and be a light in the darkness. When we live as His ambassadors, we bring His message of reconciliation into every interaction, showing others the peace and hope that only Christ can give.

Today, think about what it means to be an ambassador for Christ in your daily life. Are there relationships or situations where you can bring reconciliation or show God's love? Pray and ask God to give you the courage and wisdom to represent Him well. You don't need to have all the answers or be perfect —just a willing heart and an open spirit. Let God's grace flow through you, and trust that He will use you to make a difference in someone else's life. Let your life be a quiet prayer, a gentle offering of love that speaks God's truth even when words fall silent.

"Father, thank You for choosing me to be Your ambassador. Help me to reflect Your love and grace in every situation. Fill me with Your Spirit, so that I may bring reconciliation and hope to those around me. Give me the courage to live out my faith boldly, knowing that You are working through me. Let my life be a testament to Your goodness and mercy. In Jesus' name, Amen."

Encouragement

Remember, God chose you to be His ambassador not because of your perfection, but because of His love for you. He's empowering you to be His hands and feet, to reach out and bring others closer to Him. Stand firm in this calling, knowing that every act of kindness, every word of grace, and every moment of compassion is a step toward fulfilling God's purpose through you. Walk boldly, for God's love flows through you, and He's using you to change lives. You are a vessel of divine love, crafted to pour light into the shadows and bring warmth to weary hearts—let His purpose be the fire that moves you forward.

Choosing Whom to Serve: A Heart Fully Devoted

"No one can serve two masters. Either you will hate the one and love the other, or you will be devoted to the one and despise the other. You cannot serve both God and money."
~Matthew 6:24 (NIV)

In this powerful verse, Jesus confronts us with a choice—who will we serve? Will we let our lives be driven by the pursuit of wealth and security, or will we let God be the anchor of our hearts? Jesus knew that we'd often struggle with divided loyalty, that we'd sometimes place our trust in material things instead of in Him. But He calls us to a singular devotion, one that finds freedom in surrender and joy in trusting God as our provider. Jesus is teaching us that when our hearts are set on wealth, our focus shifts from God's purpose to our own gain. We begin to chase security in temporary things, and soon, money can become an idol, consuming our thoughts and shaping our choices. Serving money keeps us in a constant state of striving, as there's always more to acquire, more to achieve, but it never truly satisfies. God, however, offers a different kind of security—one that doesn't depend on what we own, but on who He is. When we let God be the anchor of our hearts, we find peace in His provision and the freedom to live a life that's rich in purpose, rather than possessions.

In today's world, the pressure to succeed, to gain more, and to keep up with others is intense. Society praises wealth and ambition, often equating them with worth. It's easy to fall into the trap of measuring ourselves by what we own or what we can achieve. But Jesus is warning us that living this way will only leave us empty, caught between competing desires. He knows we're not perfect, and He understands the pull of the world's values, but He also offers a better path. Serving God means placing our hope and identity in Him rather than in material success. It means prioritizing His kingdom and trusting that when we seek Him first, everything else we truly need will fall into place. True worth cannot be measured in silver or gold, for it is found in the quiet depths of a heart surrendered to love. When we let go of the world's measure, we step into a richness that cannot be bought, a peace that fills us beyond all possessions. Today, examine where your heart is invested. Are there areas where material pursuits or worries about wealth are taking the place of your devotion to God? Take a moment to surrender those things, asking God to help you realign your priorities. Choosing to serve God isn't just about giving up things—it's about gaining a life that's rich in purpose, peace, and true fulfillment. Let go of the need for control, and trust that God's provision and love will always be enough.

"Father, thank You for reminding me that You alone are my source and my strength. Help me to surrender any divided loyalties and to serve You with a fully devoted heart. Free me from the grip of materialism and the pressures of this world, and fill me with a desire to pursue Your kingdom above all else. Teach me to trust in Your provision and to find peace in Your love. In Jesus' name, Amen."

Encouragement

Remember, God knows your needs and promises to care for you as you place your trust in Him. Choosing Him over worldly pursuits brings freedom—a release from the endless cycle of wanting more. Each day you choose Him, you're building a life anchored in the only thing that can truly satisfy your soul. Stand firm in your decision to serve God wholeheartedly, knowing that He is the only master who gives peace in exchange for devotion.

Guarding Your Heart from the Love of Money

"For the love of money is a root of all kinds of evil. Some people, eager for money, have wandered from the faith and pierced themselves with many griefs."
~1 Timothy 6:10 (NIV)

This verse speaks directly to our hearts and reminds us of the danger that comes when money becomes more than a tool—it becomes our desire. Money itself isn't evil, but when it takes hold of our hearts, it begins to control our thoughts, our actions, and even our sense of worth. God, in His wisdom, knows that the love of money leads us away from true joy and fulfillment. When we let money take root in our hearts, it blinds us to the beauty of what we already have. The chase for wealth becomes an endless road, drawing us further from the stillness of contentment. God, in His love, calls us to release the grip of possession and step into the freedom of His grace. In surrendering our desire for more, we awaken to the abundance that exists in the simple, the present, the eternal. True joy is not found in accumulation, but in a heart fully alive to the richness of God's love.

In today's world, it's easy to fall into the trap of constantly seeking more. We're surrounded by messages that tell us we need the latest, the biggest, the best—and that these things define our value. But this pursuit, fueled by the love of money, can distract us from our faith and leave us feeling empty. We're not perfect; we may stumble and find ourselves caring too much about possessions or wealth. But God calls us to a higher path. When our focus shifts from the temporary to the eternal, we find a freedom that money can never buy. We begin to see wealth for what it is—a resource to be used, not a god to be served. In letting go of our grip on wealth, we discover the beauty of a heart unburdened, ready to serve and love without restraint. True richness lies not in what we own, but in what we give, and in the peace that comes from placing our trust in God alone.

Today, take inventory of your heart. Are there areas in your life where the love of money or possessions has taken priority over your relationship with God? Pray and ask Him to help you place your focus on His kingdom and not on worldly gain. Let go of the pressure to keep up or to measure yourself by what you own. Remember, true wealth is found in living a life that reflects God's love, generosity, and purpose. Therefore, lay down your pursuit of worldly riches and embrace the treasures of the spirit, for in surrendering to God's love, you will find true abundance.

"Father, thank You for reminding me of the true value of my life. Help me to guard my heart against the love of money and to trust in Your provision. Teach me to focus on what truly matters—my relationship with You, and the eternal riches found in Your love. Let me live with a spirit of generosity and contentment, knowing that I am complete in You. In Jesus' name, Amen."

Encouragement

God promises to meet our needs, to provide for us in every season. Trust in His faithfulness and know that your worth is not tied to what you own but to who you are in Him. Let your heart be anchored in His love, free from the grip of material desires. As you release the hold of wealth, you make room for a deeper, more fulfilling relationship with God. He has something far greater in store than what the world can offer.

Living Beyond the Patterns of This World

"Do not conform to the pattern of this world, but be transformed by the renewing of your mind. Then you will be able to test and approve what God's will is—His good, pleasing and perfect will."
~Romans 12:2 (NIV)

This verse is a powerful reminder that as followers of Christ, we are not meant to blend in with the values and behaviors of the world around us. Instead, God invites us to step out, to be different, to allow our minds and hearts to be reshaped by His Spirit. This verse calls us to a higher standard, a life that doesn't settle for the status quo but reaches for something greater. Transformation means embracing a mindset that isn't driven by fleeting trends or surface-level success, but by purpose, integrity, and resilience. God's Spirit empowers us to think beyond limits, to rise above the noise, and to live with clarity and conviction. Each time we choose God's way over the world's, we're rewriting our story in alignment with His vision for us. Stand out, let your life be a testament of true change, and discover the freedom that comes with a life transformed from the inside out.

In today's world, it's easy to get swept up in the constant noise —social media, peer pressure, and cultural expectations all push us to think and act in ways that often go against what God has for us. We're told to seek approval, chase after success, and define our worth by what we accomplish or possess. But God knows that when we align our thoughts and desires with the world, we miss out on His best for us. He doesn't expect us to be perfect, but He does invite us to open our hearts and minds to His transforming power. Through His Spirit, He renews our thoughts, shifting our focus from temporary pursuits to eternal truths. This is the transformation He calls us to—a mind and heart that seek His will above all else. Step away from the world's clamor, and you'll find a whisper of truth within, guiding you to a life beyond the ordinary. In His hands, your heart becomes a canvas, painted with purpose and eternal beauty, a reflection of His boundless love. Today, examine areas in your life where you might be conforming to the world's standards. Are there influences or habits that keep you from fully embracing God's purpose for you? Pray and ask Him to help renew your mind, to replace worldly desires with a heart that seeks Him first. Surrender the pressure to fit in, and let God's truth shape your perspective. Embracing transformation isn't always easy, but it leads to a life that is rooted in His peace and clarity.

"Father, thank You for calling me to a life of transformation. Help me to resist the pull of worldly patterns and to seek Your will with a renewed heart and mind. Fill me with Your Spirit, and guide my thoughts and actions to align with Your truth. Let my life be a reflection of Your love, grace, and purpose. In Jesus' name, Amen."

Encouragement

Remember, God's will for you is good, pleasing, and perfect. As you allow Him to renew your mind, you'll begin to see His purpose unfold in ways that go beyond anything the world can offer. Stand firm in His truth, and trust that each step toward transformation brings you closer to the life He designed for you. Walk boldly in this newness, knowing that God's path leads to true freedom, joy, and fulfillment. Embrace each day as a step closer to His heart, letting His light guide you through the shadows of doubt and fear. Trust that even in the smallest acts of faith, you are woven into a purpose far greater than you can imagine.

Go out into the world with a heart full of grace, for you are the light that can brighten even the darkest of places. Be kind in a world that often forgets the beauty of kindness; lift others up, for in doing so, you lift yourself. Leave a trail of compassion wherever you walk, speak words that heal, and give more than you take. Each moment you choose to love, to help, to encourage, you bring heaven closer to earth. Let your spirit be a quiet balm in the chaos, a reminder to all who meet you that goodness is alive, and it flows through the hearts willing to give.

Made in United States
Orlando, FL
27 November 2024